THE ART OF
PATCHWORK

By the same author:
Drawn Fabric Embroidery (Batsford, 1979)

THE ART OF PATCHWORK

Edna Wark

LAROUSSE & CO., INC.

Acknowledgements

This book could not have been written without: Elsie, who started me off; Will, who supported it; Susan, who typed the manuscript; Barbara, who participated in it; Friends who lent their work for it; The Embroiderers' Guild, Victoria, Australia, who co-operated with it, and Dee Starr who photographed it. I thank them all most sincerely.

In particular, I would like to thank the following for allowing me to use their patchwork to illustrate my text: Doreen Bates, figure 61 (fitted work box); Louise Body, figure 48; Elsie Clark, figure 9; Janice Clyne, figure 12; Beryl Dean and Elizabeth Elvin, figure 52; Judy Esdaile, figure 5 (pincushion with velvet ribbon and pincushion with emery powder) and 59; Rene Foers, figure 5 (pincushion with wristband); Gillian Gowers, figure 54; E. M. John, figure 53 and colour plate 5; Val Landmann, figures 41 and 47; Margaret Lindell, figure 18; Joan Lynch, figures 25 and 35; Barbara Macey, figures 43, 44, 45 and colour plates 3 and 4; Audrey McMahon, back jacket photo; J. Rijs, figure 56; Wendy Ritchie, figures 26, 60, and 61 (wooden box with inset nursery figures) and Leslie Watts, colour plates 1 and 2.

My grateful thanks also to the following collections for permission to reproduce photographs: Embroiderers' Guild Collection, figures 30 and 49; National Gallery of Victoria, Melbourne, Australia, figure 33; Worthing Museum, figure 36 and Victoria and Albert Museum, London, figure 51. Thanks also to the following individuals who loaned me pieces of patchwork for use in this book: Dorothea Alnutt, figure 20; Morna Sturrock, figure 53 and Rene Foers, figure 62.

First published 1984

First published in the U.S.A. by
Larousse & Co., Inc.
572 Fifth Avenue
New York, N.Y. 10036

ISBN 0–88332–330–3

Library of Congress No. 83–48903

Printed in Great Britain

Contents

Foreword

You may well ask 'Is there any need for yet another book on patchwork?' and I would be tempted to sympathize with you, but my experience as a teacher of courses for adult education groups made up largely of women of mature age and young mums, is such that I must say 'Yes'. One of my colleagues said to me: 'If you are going to write a book on patchwork please put into it all those helpful hints that we give to students and which are not considered of sufficient importance to print.'

So this is my justification. I have written this book to satisfy my teaching requirements and, I hope, the needs of many who do not have ready access to specialist teachers or libraries equipped with all the necessary volumes from which to cull the assorted bits of information that experience accumulates.

Introduction

My original teacher was a lady of nearly 80 who in her long lifetime had become proficient in many branches of crafts, and her teaching was definite and knowledgeable – no half measures. Patchwork was a precise form and there should be no skimping in the way of perfect finish and nothing slovenly in the construction.

Patchwork is at its best when supplies are limited to what is to hand, because then one has really to work at the design and the results are better thought out. This does not mean that it is not permissible to buy materials, but the essential personality of patchwork tends to be lost if quantities of new material are purchased for a project. There is the sentimental attachment that goes with patchwork when pieces are the bits from treasured friends or traded through close associations. Patchwork has been done in many parts of the world from Egypt to the Arctic, so obviously the range of materials that has been used is large.

For centuries patchwork was done by hand – there was no alternative – but now some beautiful pieces are made by machine, although the designs of machine-made patchwork involve restraints inherent in the method. The skirt (*figure 67*) was made by machine in this instance but has also been made by hand by students and it is, I think, easier to keep the diamonds absolutely true when done in this manner.

In my courses we take a different geometric shape for each session and make a small item, so that at the end of the course every student has worked with a variety of shapes and all have a selection of small articles to take away.

The projects in this book, though based on the items done in these courses, go well beyond those that can be completed in a few hours.

These items may not be highly original, but serve to demonstrate how important the choice of colour is in designing patchwork; how simple it is to use some shapes and how complex other shapes, with their complementary shapes, can be.

Later, it may not be necessary to work with the same size template all the time (e.g. some shapes combine to make other simple, larger shapes which add interest) and economy of time can thus be achieved by thoughtful planning (*figure 66*) and, with basic understanding of the shapes and what can be done with them, it is possible to adapt standard shapes to fit into particular needs (*figure 26*), or use the same shapes in a variety of sizes (*colour plate 7*)

One must be very experienced to produce the wonderfully sophisticated works that are made by Barbara Macey (*figures 43, 44 and 45*). Some of her panels are vividly coloured, but all-black ones, using a wide variety of materials are beautiful and subtle. Unfortunately, the all-black ones do not photograph well. The effects she can achieve by using one fabric only and by playing with the light reflected from materials cut in different directions is eye-catching and breath-taking. They are all based on the Log Cabin principle.

The sections of this book will take readers through various kinds of patchwork, using a different geometric shape in each section and, unless otherwise stated, in each case we will use a 1 in. (2·5 cm) template.

If you use felt for your patchwork it is not necessary to have extra material for turnings. In this case you can do your stitching on the right side, if you wish, and use running stitch, overcasting or glove stitch (*figure 7*). In patchwork made from fabric the pieces are usually sewn together with top-stitching, or over-casting, working from the back of the work. Contemporary American patchwork is commonly done by joining the patches by machine, or with hand-sewn seams using running stitch. Much of it is concerned with applied designs on squares of material which are then sewn together.

I do not intend to do more than make passing references to contemporary American patchwork. It is a large field of which I have only a slight knowledge and there are many books devoted to the subject, some of which I have included in the Bibliography at the end of this book.

1 Basic Principles

1 You need a template.

2 You cut paper shapes from this template. They must be exactly the same size as the template. These are called 'papers' or 'cards', although they are not cut from cardboard.

3 You cut a piece of material from your template allowing ¼ in. (6 mm) turnings all round.

4 You tack your fabric to the papers, turning over the seam allowance and making the corner folds of the same material as sharp and crisp as possible.

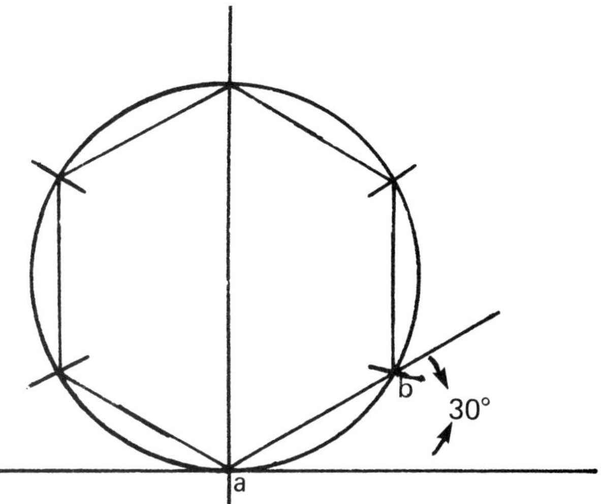

Diagram 1 *How to obtain a hexagon template (method 1).*

Templates

Commercially cut templates are usually metal and sometimes come with a plastic 'window' complete with extra amount equal to the required fabric turning. In this case you cut your fabric from this 'window' and exactly this size. If you can find, or cut, clear plastic templates you do not need both template and 'window'. The advantage of plastic templates is that you can see the pattern on the material which is an asset if you are trying to centre a spot or a flower. But do not get ones in plastic which are more than ⅛ in. (3 mm) thick, if cutting with scissors. Some scissors have blades that will not cut properly if resting against a thick template. If cutting with a razor blade it would be no trouble.

There is much to be said for cutting your own templates if you are mathematically minded, but with the very good range of commercially made templates on the market today it needs an enthusiast or an unusual demand to do it at home. The time is always likely to arise, however, when you will not have a template of a size and shape to fit into a pattern on which you are working.

Hexagons, pentagons and octagons

Basically the hexagon, pentagon and the octagon are derived from a circle and, if you intend to use only one of them, it is relatively simple. If, however, you will be using several shapes in conjunction the length of the sides of all of them *must* match. This will not be the case if the radius of the circle used is the same in each case. The following table should be of help.

Length of side	*Radii of circle*		
	HEXAGON	OCTAGON	PENTAGON
0·75 in. (1·9 cm)	0·75 in. (1·9 cm)	0·98 in. (2·5 cm)	0·64 in. (1·16 cm)
1 in. (2·5 cm)	1 in. (2·5 cm)	1·31 in. (3·32 cm)	0·85 in. (2·15 cm)
1·50 in. (3·81 cm)	1·50 in. (3·81 cm)	1·96 in. (5 cm)	1·28 in. (3·25 cm)

Method 1

This is the method which is usually recommended and requires that you draw a base line and one cutting it at right angles.

a For the hexagon:
Draw a circle of appropriate radius (refer to Table above) with the centre point on the perpendicular line and the edge of the circle on the base line. Draw a line at 30 degrees from the point of intersection of the base line and the perpendicular line and continue until it meets the circle (*diagram 1*). Open your compass to the length of the line between intersections **a** and **b**. Mark off this length in successive steps around the circumference and you will have six points which, when joined, give the six sides of the hexagon. (Incidentally, it will probably be found that the accuracy of your drawing is improved if the centre of every pair of lines is marked with a pin prick where they intersect, before using the compass.)

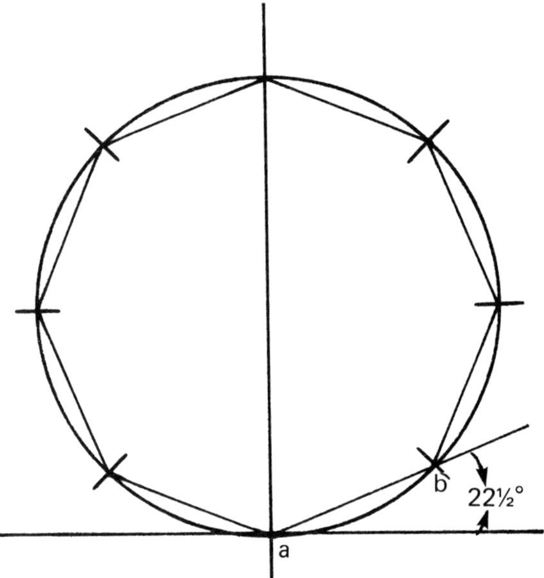

Diagram 2 *How to obtain an octagon template (method 1).*

b For the octagon:
Start in the same way using the circle of appropriate radius (refer to Table). The angle at the base point is, however, 22½ degrees in this case and the compass, opened to the distance between the intersections **a** and **b** will, in successive steps, mark the eight points of the octagon (*diagram 2*).

c For the pentagon:
Use the same method and you will find that a base angle of 36 degrees will give a pentagon with the desired length of side from the appropriate circle (*diagram 3*).

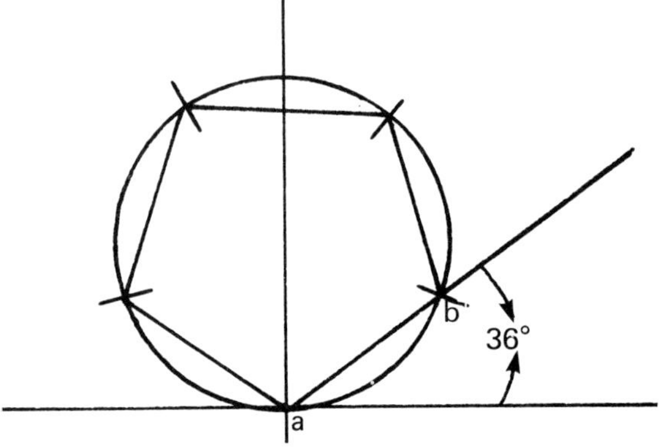

Diagram 3 *How to obtain a pentagon template (method 1).*

Method 2

I include another method of deriving the shapes for these templates. I think it is preferable

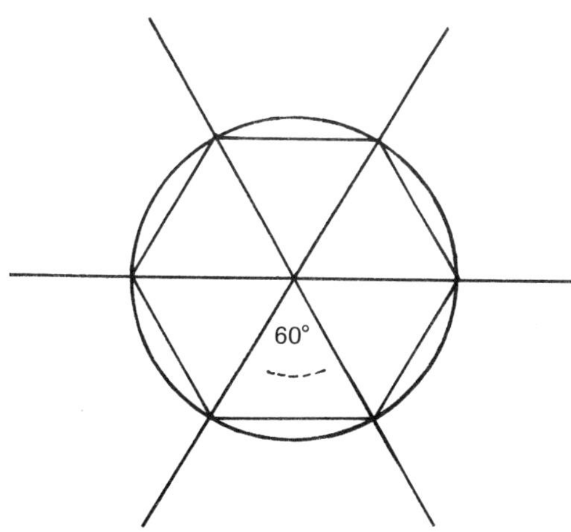

Diagram 4 *How to obtain a hexagon template (method 2).*

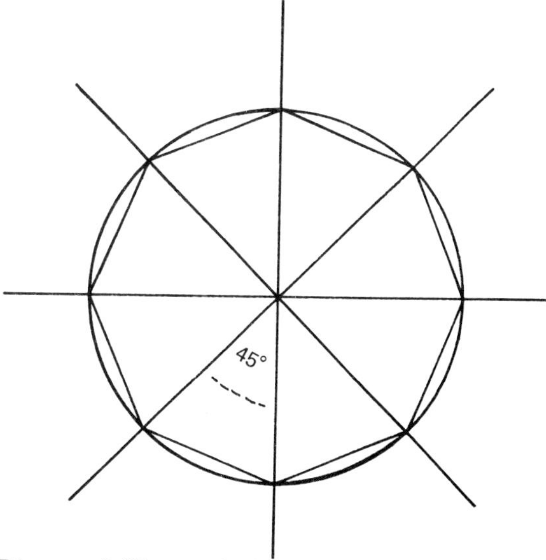

Diagram 5 *How to obtain an octagon template (method 2).*

because I seem to obtain more accurate results, but stress that, in both methods it is the accuracy of measuring the angles which is vital.

a For the hexagon:
Rule a horizontal line, and two other lines all crossing at a central point. The six angles thus formed must all measure 60 degrees. Draw a circle with appropriate radius (refer to Table) using this centre point and the six points of intersection with the lines will, when joined, give you the six sides of your hexagon (*diagram 4*).

b For the octagon:
Use a similar method but having four crossing lines at an angle of 45 degrees to one another. A circle of appropriate radius will give the points of the desired octagon (refer to Table and diagram 5).

c For the pentagon:
The method is again similar. In this case, however, start by marking a central point and draw a horizontal line d–e from it, in one direction only. Then draw lines, but *not crossing*, only meeting at the centre point, at 72 degrees and 144 degrees on either side of this line (*diagram 6*). The appropriate size of circle will give the desired pentagon (refer to Table and diagram 6).

I prefer this second method because it is easier to find the point where the radiating lines

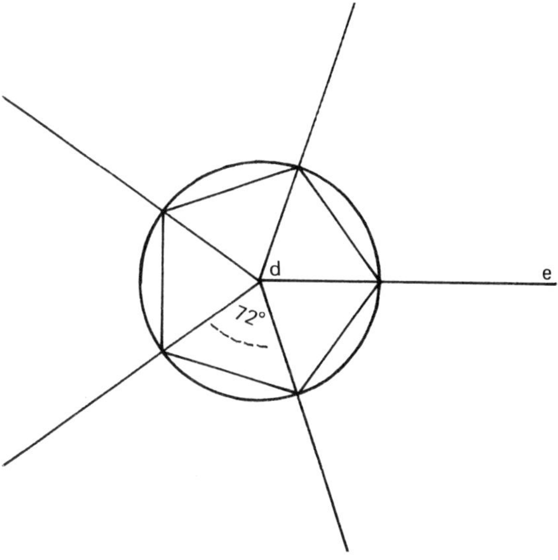

Diagram 6 *How to obtain a pentagon template (method 2).*

cross the circumference when they do it at an angle which is nearly square, rather than the more commonly used method where the angle at the circumference is much more acute.

Squares, rectangles and triangles

These can be made with the aid of a ruler, a protractor and/or a square. Once again, the best accuracy can probably be obtained if the centre of each intersection of two lines is identified by means of a pin point and other lines and angles are ruled through or centred on this point.

Material and method

Light-weight perspex or celluloid sheet makes satisfactory templates. Draw the shape on strong paper and cut it out. Attach it to the underside of the perspex with sticking tape and place on a piece of mirror. With someone holding the perspex, cut along the lines of the shape with a craft knife pressed firmly against the edge of a steel ruler. The edge of the resultant template will need smoothing with a file or fine sand paper.

Checking the templates for accuracy

This can be done:

a by measuring the actual lengths of *all* sides and the angles; or

b by comparing the lengths of *all* sides of one paper with those of another.

It is a good idea to compare the shapes of two papers by superimposing them in several ways.

Even metal templates wear down with constant, prolonged use.

Cutting papers

a You can cut around your template while holding the template and paper between your finger and thumb, using scissors, or

b you can place the paper with the template on top of a piece of old mirror and cut around with a razor blade or craft knife.

In either case your cutting *must* be accurate as the entire finish of your patchwork can be ruined if your papers have been badly cut.

If cutting with scissors, do not attempt to cut more than two layers of paper at once. More than that and they are likely to slip.

Use good quality paper with print on it, not newsprint. Company reports are very good, as are also technical journals.

Cut the papers with lines of print running parallel to one side of the template when using hexagons, octagons or squares. If the lines of print are then placed on the grain of the fabric pieces you need not worry when you are joining patches together which way the grain is running. The lines will tell you. This is a great help when working with dark-coloured patches.

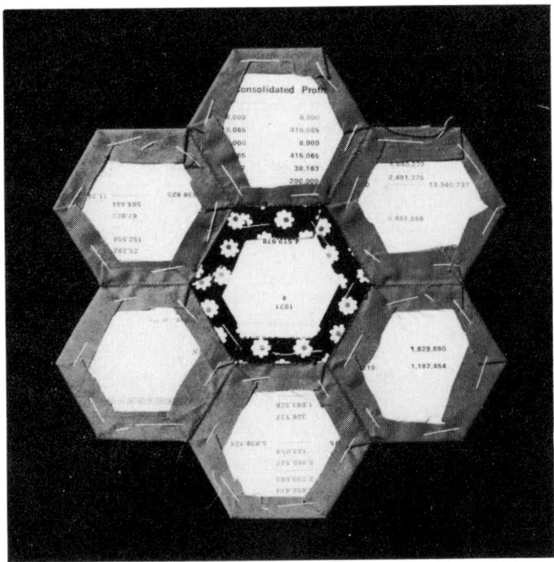

Figure 1 *Lines of print on papers can be very helpful.*

Make sure you keep a separate pair of scissors for this purpose, as cutting paper will blunt them very quickly.

Cutting patches

Use your template to cut out the fabric; the 'window' template gives you the exact size, inclusive of the fabric turning required. The two most important points to notice when cutting out patches are the pattern on the material itself, and the direction of the grain of the fabric. If in doubt as to which is the grain, pull a thread from the edge before commencing to cut.

It is important to make a habit of seeing that the grain on the fabric runs vertically and horizontally. Your patches will sit better and, when making a large piece (e.g. a quilt), it will hang better. It is also important if you are using silks or synthetics or other materials with a sheen. The sheen varies with the direction of the woven threads. Of course, with experience, it is possible to use one kind of material only and achieve your pattern by cutting the pieces so that the sheen *does* vary.

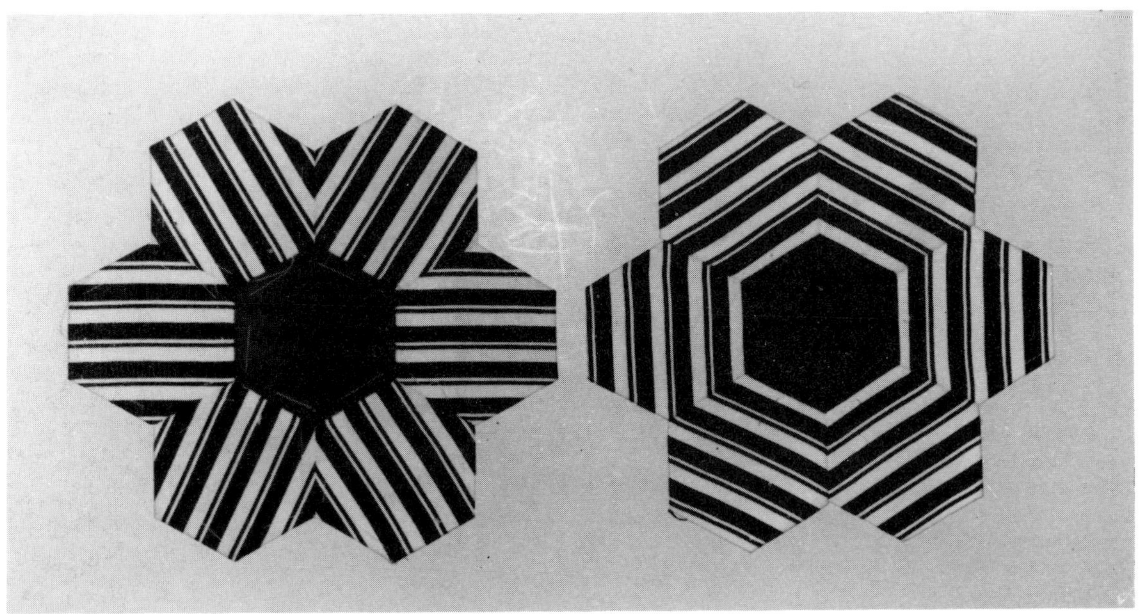

Figure 2 *Two ways of using stripes for hexagon flower motifs. Cutting and matching of stripes must be very accurate.*

There are other exceptions to this rule – for example, when you need to use stripes as a part of your design (*figure 2*). In cases such as these, you plan the direction of the stripes and make sure that everything else *is* on the grain. (For a more detailed description of making the most of the pattern and colouring of materials, see Chapter 4.)

If your work appears to be suffering from lack of precision, you will need to check the template.

Tacking papers to material

Hold a 'paper' and a piece of material together with a single pin while you become used to tacking papers to material.

When tacking the papers to the fabric it is sufficient to pierce the material with the needle midway along each side and at the corners, unless the sides of the patches are more than 2 in. (5 cm) long. When tacking fabric to papers, keep the knot on the *right* side of the work when making a flat piece. (For a further explanation of the reasons for this, *see p. 96.*) If making something that finally will be turned inside out, have knots on the *wrong* side of the work.

If all layers are carefully folded at the corners they will be caught in the stitch. Unnecessary stitches are a waste of time, but the fabric must be securely caught. A single back stitch is usually enough to fasten the thread.

To centre a spot or flower when tacking patches to papers, fold your paper in half lengthways, then in half across and snip the folded tip. You can then place the hole carefully over the detail to give the centre.

Diamond shapes present a special problem when tacking them to papers. You will notice that two points are much sharper than the other two. The traditional way to fold the material at the sharp corners is to fold it flat across the top, then turn one side down and then the other. This makes the point rather bulky. Another way to do it is to turn one side over the paper right to the point, then turn the other side over. There will be an ear standing out (*figure 3*).

When you are ready to sew two patches together hold the extended piece back under your thumb or forefinger, as the case may be, and sew the two edges together as usual. Then let the projecting piece or 'ear' lie back, and when all six points are joined in the centre of a star they will press flat on the wrong side and be much less bulky.

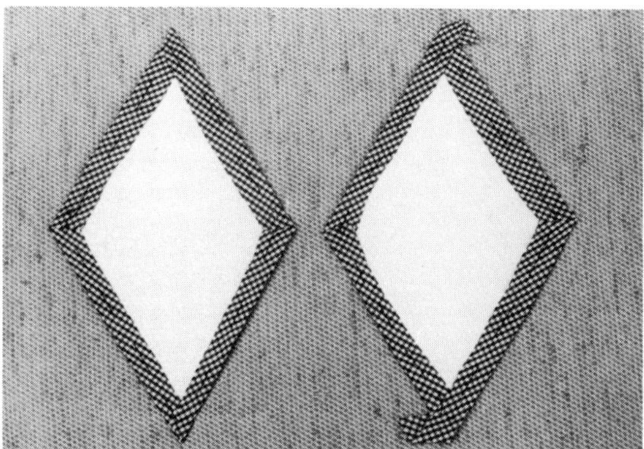

Figure 3 *The seam allowance on diamond patches can be folded in two different ways depending on where they are to be used.*

This method is only useful when the work is 'pieced'. If the stars made from diamonds are to be 'applied' to a ground the older method must be used at the outer points so that they may be stitched tidily to the background.

Joining patches

After the fabric has been tacked to the papers the patches are sewn together by oversewing along the edges (right sides facing and only along one side to begin with). Just the very edge threads of the fabric should be taken up in these stitches – *never* should the stitches penetrate the edges of the papers. When opened out your patches should lie flat side by side. If your stitches are big enough to take up the edge of the papers there will be a ridge in the seam and as well as not sitting flat there will be an alteration to the size of the patch. It will be only a small amount of difference, but multiplied over and over again, it will cause a noticeable discrepancy.

Needles and threads

Use a fine, small needle. 'Betweens' size 9 are a good buy. If you are unfamiliar with 'Betweens', they are shorter than 'Sharps' or 'Crewels' and you will find that you will make much smaller stitches than usual. You *can* make small stitches with a large needle but you *cannot* make big stitches with a small needle.

Although minute stitches are not necessary, about 12 stitches to 1 in. (2·5 cm) is a good working average to aim for.

For joining your patches use cotton thread – only use synthetic thread if you are solely using synthetic materials. Sheen no. 50, or finer, is quite suitable. No. 90 used to be the recommended thickness but it is very rare today.

Traditionally patchwork is sewn with black or white thread. I feel that this must go back to the time when only black or white was available, for I can see no reason why, if you are sewing pink floral material to plain pink material, you cannot use pink thread.

It is a fact, however, that dark cotton shows less on the light material (if you are joining a light and a dark) than white cotton does on a dark ground. Anyway, if your stitches only penetrate the edge threads of your patches they will be practically lost in the texture of the material in any case.

Waxing the thread is a good idea; it strengthens it and helps keep it from tangling. Lightly draw the thread over a piece of beeswax. If you draw the thread deeply into the wax, too much will adhere and it will 'cloud' the thread. I find the most satisfactory wax is that used by tailors who still do their buttonholes by hand. It is obtainable from tailors' suppliers.

Do not use a thread that is more than 16–18 in. (40–50 cm) long. I always tie a single knot $\frac{1}{2}$ in. (1·25 cm) from the end of the thread. I pull the threaded needle through the material until the knot is reached, then I hold the tail of cotton against the patches and sew over the tail as I progress with my stitching. This way the end will not come loose and the knot is quite invisible (*figure 4*). (When tacking it is quite acceptable to knot the end of the thread.)

To finish off, a couple of back stitches or one or two stitches on top of each other and the end run into the seam, works well.

With the papers accurately cut and material carefully tacked, sides of patches should always match neatly. It is no good trying to ease patches together; if they are not accurate, they will *never* sit correctly. Corners must always butt onto each other. Work well done, when held up to the light, will not show holes where the corners meet.

Figure 4 *Starting to stitch. Shows method of starting with a knot and stitches holding tail of cotton firmly on seam.*

Patchwork shapes, in most cases, have straight sides. This is because, in the beginning, they were cut in the hand with scissors, from folded pieces of paper. It is harder – but not impossible – to join seams that are curved, in the manner of patchwork. Usually the designs with curved outlines are applied.

Once the patches are sewn together the tacking threads can be snipped and the papers removed.

Do not discard papers after use. They can be used again and again until they become worn and inaccurate.

Planning patchwork

The most satisfactory materials to use for patchwork are colour-fast cottons, similar in weight to poplin or lawn. *Always* wash cottons before use. You will spend a lot of time making your project and you do not want the pieces to shrink unevenly, nor bleed colour, after completion. (If it bleeds colour, discard it!)

To begin with, a mixture of plain and patterned fabrics is usually stimulating and satisfying (*figure 5*). Everyone has his or her own personality and this comes out in patchwork; some will be gay, some sombre. In the early stages, beware too much variety, although some people can use the most amazing mixture of patterned fabrics and get away with it.

For articles that are to be washed, avoid mixing cottons, synthetics and pile fabrics. Widely varied materials come into their own in two forms of patchwork that are quite different in construction to those done with templates: Crazy and Log Cabin patchwork. These are covered in Chapters 4 and 6.

In the USA, where the patchwork tradition was taken by the early settlers from England and Europe, it became a way of life. Quilting parties were a definite part of the social pattern. Their quilts were known as 'patched' or 'pieced'. It is the 'pieced' quilts that we know as patchwork. The 'patched' ones were fabric patterns applied onto a ground fabric. There are instances where both techniques are used to complement each other.

A wonderful source of patchwork patterns are the tiles on floors and verandahs of houses built in the Victorian era. Even contemporary mosaic tiles on bathroom floors have many colour schemes suitable for patchwork.

When making a large piece of work do not commence with the patch in the dead centre and for ever after work around and around it. Try to plan your work so that you can do it in sections, joining finished sections as you go, and finally join two pieces to finish the job.

There is a lot to be said for making a quilt as a winter project – it does keep the knees warm as it grows!

The shapes

The commonly used shapes are: hexagon, octagon, square and other rectangles. To these may be added: pentagon, elongated pentagon, hexagon diamond, octagon diamond, church window, equilateral triangle, circle and clamshell.

For beginners I must stress that when using a

Figure 5 *Two examples of hexagon flower motifs.*

variety of shapes together it is the length of the side of the templates that is important. They *must* all measure the same, e.g. 1 in. (2·5 cm), $1\frac{1}{2}$ in. (3·8 cm), or whatever other measurement you are working with.

With experience it is possible to build up complicated patterns using combinations of sizes (*figure 26*).

It will prove worthwhile if, initially, you make the first four or five examples given in the following pages in a variety of colour combinations and different fabrics to familiarize yourself with the techniques.

2 Geometric patches with straight edges

The hexagon

I always use this shape as the first lesson because the shapes fit together – they lie flat with no extra shapes needed, and there is more than one colour interpretation of the basic 'flower' motif possible (*figure 6*). In making this motif you must think of colour as well as pattern.

To make one flower motif you need to cut seven papers from the template. Select your fabrics for:

1 a plain fabric for the centre surrounded by six patterned ones; or

2 a patterned fabric for the centre surrounded by six plain ones; or

3 a plain coloured one for the centre surrounded by six different plain colours; or

4 a plain coloured one for the centre surrounded by two different plain colours placed alternately; or

5 a plain or patterned one for the centre and alternate plain and patterned ones around it.

One motif lined with old blanket or felt and a back attached makes a pot holder. Bind the layers together around the edge.

Two pincushions (*figure 6*)

Two motifs can be joined around the outer edges and stuffed to make a pincushion.

Two motifs with a piece of velvet ribbon inserted in the edge, as a wall, and then stuffed makes another kind of pincushion.

For both types of pincushion cut 14 fabric patches in one of the above combinations – remember to allow turnings.

Sew fabric to papers. Join seven hexagons to make a flower.

Repeat with the other seven hexagons. Reverse the colour placing in the second piece, if you wish, but decide this before cutting your patches.

In making pincushions it is not necessary to press your patchwork as the stuffing process will smooth it out and it is unlikely that, in making only one flower, it will become crushed.

To assemble the pincushion

1 Place the two completed pieces together with the right sides facing each other. Oversew the edges together but leave three edges of one patch open so that you may turn the pincushion inside out and insert the stuffing.

Remove the tacking and take out papers carefully. (I find a coarse plastic knitting needle is a great help in taking out the tackings.)

Tack the edges of the opening carefully so that they will not stretch.

Turn the pincushion inside out. Carefully pull the corners out.

The ideal stuffing for pincushions is fleece wool but if this is not available use synthetic filling such as dacron or acrylic pillow stuffing. Insert the stuffing in small amounts and push it into the farthest corners first. Continue stuffing until the pincushion is firm and nearly filled.

Figure 6 *Group of pincushions.*
Top row from left to right:
pincushion with a wall and central stitching; pincushion without a wall; pincushion with a wristband of tiny hexagons enclosing elastic.
Bottom row from left to right:
pincushion with a wall of velvet ribbon and a loop; tiny pincushion containing emery powder.

Start closing the opening, stuffing more as you go until it is firm.

It is surprising how much stuffing is needed in such a small article. It should be very firm to keep its shape.

If you wish to have a hanger on your pincushion place a loop of ribbon in the seam before you close it.

2 If you wish to make a pincushion with a wall, remove papers after you have made two flowers. Tack all edges carefully – being especially careful with the corners – then proceed to sew the ribbon or braid along the edges. Make your stitching on the right side. If using a 1 in. (2·5 cm) template, 20 in. ($\frac{1}{2}$ m) of velvet ribbon or woven braid is sufficient for the wall, but $\frac{1}{2}$ yd (45 cm) is not quite enough.

You can either:

a sew the ribbon or braid all the way around the flower and then mark each corner with a pin and sew the other flower to the other side of the ribbon or braid with the corners corresponding. Use top-sewing or glove stitch. Or,

b using a separate needle and thread for each side of the wall, sew along one section, then using the other needle sew along the corresponding edge on the other side of the wall. Continue until nearly all the way around. Leave an opening for stuffing.

The corners *must* match on either side of the wall, otherwise the pincushion takes on a peculiar, twisted shape.

There must be *no* fullness in the wall.

Finally stuff the pincushion and then seam the join in the wall.

It is most important to ensure that there is sufficient stuffing in this pincushion.

Optional finish

I like to make firm stitches right through the pincushion around the centre hexagon. It helps

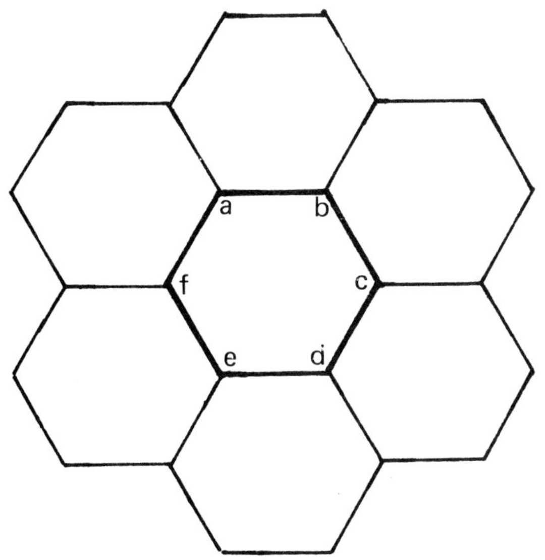

Diagram 7 *Hexagon pincushion showing the central stitching lines.*

to keep the pincushion in shape and very firm (*diagram 7*).

The stitching is done in two stages. Thread a coarse toning thread (e.g. no. 5 Pearl thread) into a darning needle. Come through the pincushion at **a** leaving 3 to 4 in. (8 to 10 cm) hanging behind. Go down at **b**, up at **c**, down at **d**, up at **e** and down at **f**. Pull the thread tight and tie a reef knot; then take the needle through the pincushion. Pull thread tight and cut off. It will run back out of sight. Thread the other end of the cotton into the needle and get rid of it in the same way.

Now with the same thick cotton fill in the gaps. Come through the pincushion at **b**, down at **c**, up at **d**, down at **e**, up at **f** and down at **a**. Finish ends as before.

The elongated pentagon

I include this shape at this point because it is much more closely related to the hexagon than to the pentagon. It is cut from a hexagon. Eliminate one side and extend the adjacent sides of the eliminated one until they join (*diagram 8*). When six are joined together they make a flower similar to that made by seven hexagons.

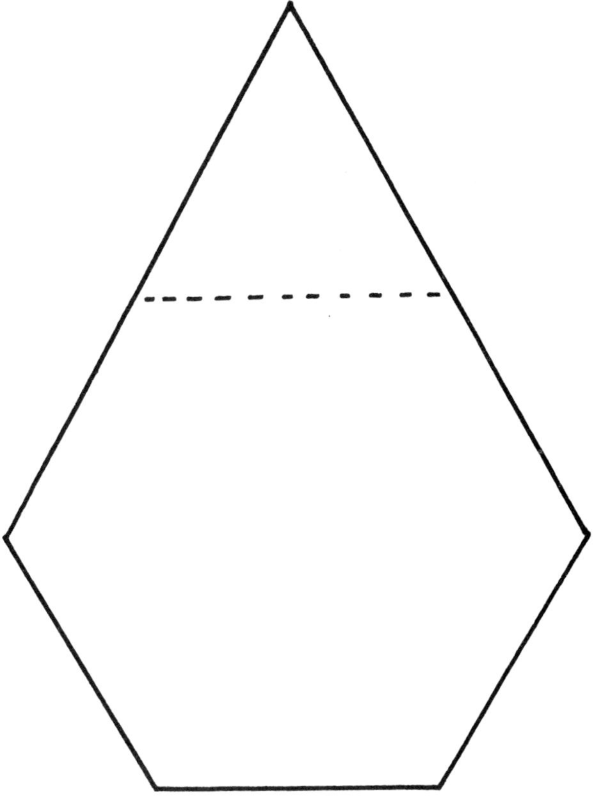

Diagram 8 *How to obtain an elongated pentagon from a hexagon.*

The pentagon

Used by themselves these shapes do not make a flat piece. Five patches joined together around a central one make a bowl-shaped object. Two of these joined together make a ball.

A ball (*figure 7*)

Cut 12 papers. (There is no need for papers if you are using felt.)

Select fabrics. One or two varieties, but no more. (You cannot have alternating fabrics around the centre patch because you have five patches in the ring.)

Cut 12 pentagon patches (with turnings, unless you are using felt which does not fray). Tack fabric patches to papers. Join the centre patch and five others.

Repeat with the other patches. You will then have two bowl-shaped structures. Join these two pieces together so that the points of one half

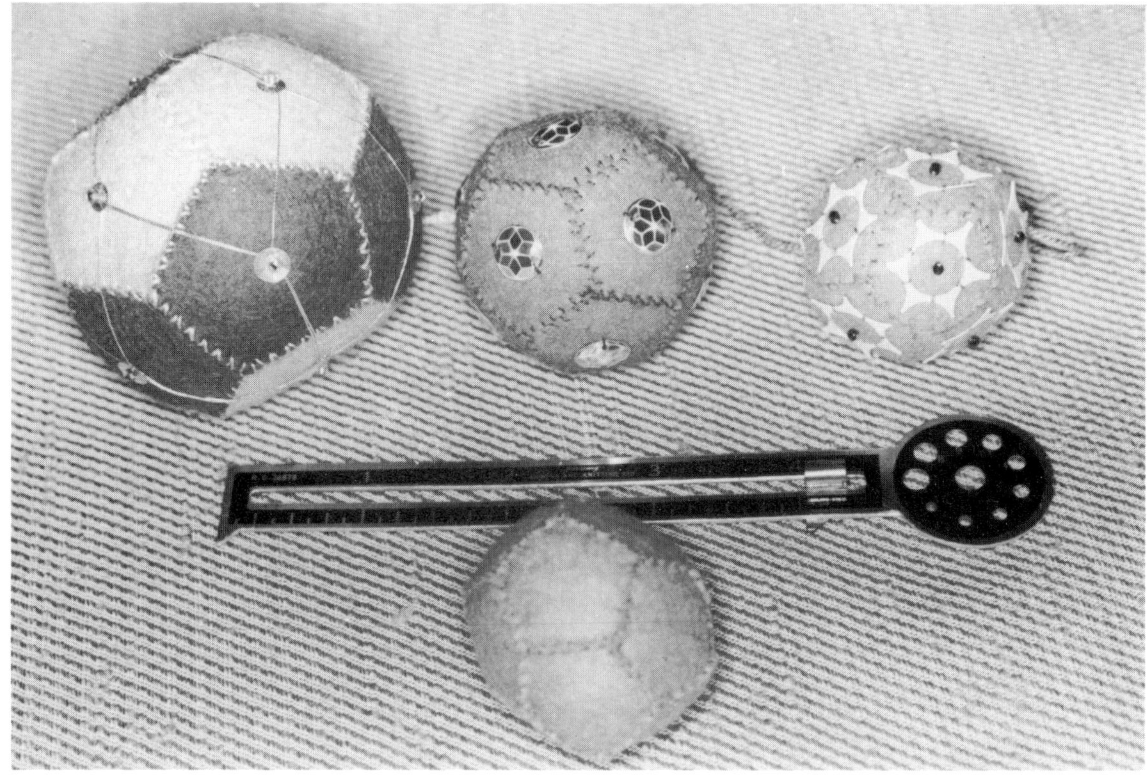

Figure 7 *Pentagon balls made in felt. Gauge measures 4 in. (10 cm). Note the way the pieces fit into each other and glove stitching.*

fit into the hollows of the other. (Do this from the wrong side, except when using felt.) Leave an opening.

Take out papers. Tack edges of fabric patches left for opening. Turn inside out.

Stuff with filling, moulding it into a ball as you stuff. Sew opening together with invisible stitching.

This makes a lovely baby's toy when made in washable fabrics. Very small ones are good ornaments for a Christmas tree. They can be decorated with beads or tinsel threads. Do this before joining the patches.

If using felt, cut patches without turnings and stitch on the right side using overcasting or glove stitch.

The octagon

Many beautiful patterns use the octagon which combines well with certain other shapes. It needs the square to fill in the blanks in the simplest arrangement.

It is always a surprise to see how big an octagon is, even with $\frac{1}{2}$ in. (1·25 cm) sides, and it seems to grow tremendously for every size larger.

In the example given, squares and church windows are added. To make a church window take an octagon paper and fold it very carefully making a crisp line from **a** to **b** (*diagram 9*). Keep the paper folded and carefully cut around the edge of the paper, discarding the shaded area of the octagon paper. All the edges will be the same length as in the original octagon so the sides will still fit together.

A spectacle case to hold two pairs

(*figure 8*)

Cut 18 octagon papers. From six of these cut church windows. Cut 21 square papers with the same length of side as the octagons.

Select fabrics. Three different ones can be used. You will need a lot more fabric for the octagons than the squares or church windows.

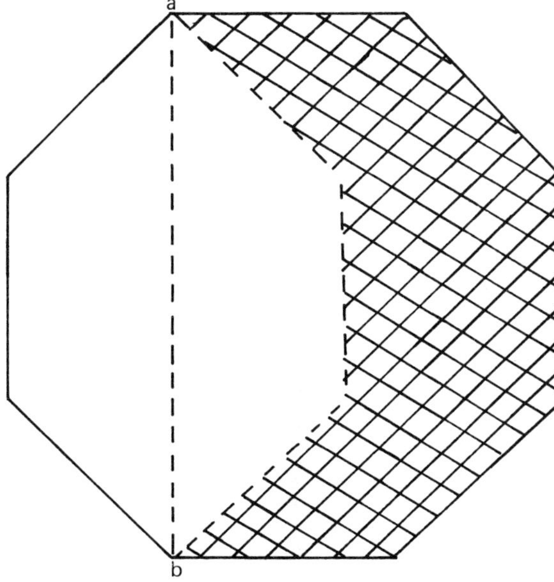

Diagram 9 *How to obtain a church window from an octagon.*

Cut patches (in shapes matching the papers) with turnings. Tack patches to papers.

Join 14 squares to the church windows and then join octagons to squares and church windows.

Fold this strip in half, lengthwise, and try your spectacles inside for size. This strip will be about $14\frac{1}{2}$ in. (37 cm) in length.

Remove papers and tack edges so they will not stretch.

Cut a piece of wadding to fit your patchwork strip. Pin in place and quilt centre panel – church windows and squares. (Quilting is small, even running stitches in lines just inside the stitching lines which join the patches. It is subtly decorative and holds the wadding firmly in place.)

Figure 8 *Octagon spectacle case which holds two pairs.*

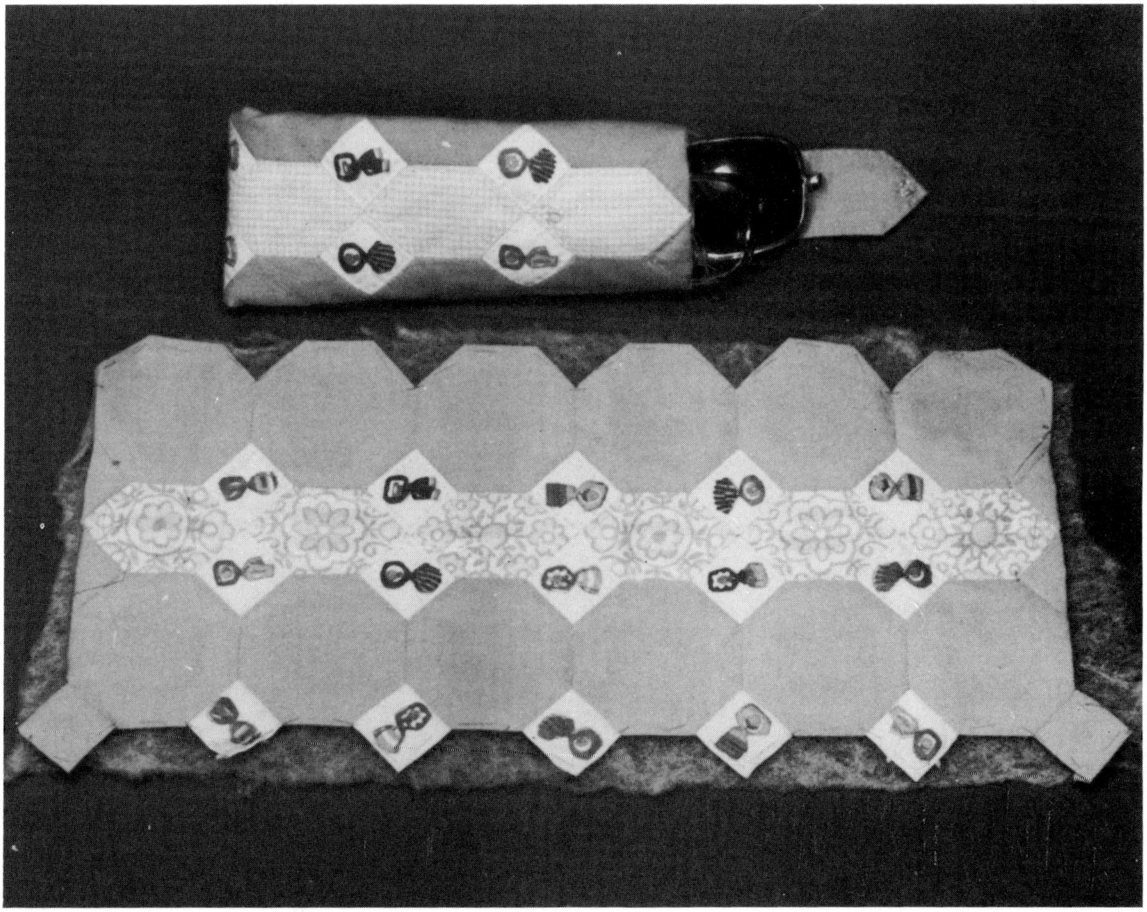

Trim wadding so that it is the same size as the patchwork and catch together.

Join edges of patchwork to make a tube. The shapes will fit into each other. It is easiest to do the stitching on the outside but make it as inconspicuous as possible. When the tube is folded in half, so that there are two pockets for spectacles, these stitches do not show.

Lining

Make a lining of soft silk. It should be a straight strip the same size as your completed patchwork, plus turnings. Seam along the long edge so it exactly fits inside your patchwork tube.

Depending on whether or not you are making a flap fastening, turn down protruding points on one or both ends of the patchwork tube.

If you wish to put a flap on the case to prevent the glasses from falling out, now is the time to do it. Make it to match the pattern of the patchwork. An extra church window can be cut with longer sides than the others to make the flap. Interline with vilene, or similar stiffening, and line with silk to match the lining of the case. Join to case between two projecting squares.

Place lining inside tube of patchwork and slip stitch to patchwork at either end.

Fold in half so that church windows form a line of pattern on the outside of the tube.

You only need now to stitch the ends of the tube together where they meet and you have a case which will take two pairs of spectacles or a pair of spectacles and a pair of sunglasses. Add fastenings to the flap.

The square

The simplest geometric shape used in patchwork is the square and it is most suitable for machined work; when correctly cut on the grain of the material there is never any doubt as to which way the patches should go. If possible, tear your material, leaving ¼ in. (6 mm) turnings on all sides.

1 *using a machine:* select your colours, join the patches into strips, then join the strips. Press the seams in each strip before joining the strips together. All seams should join accurately.

2 *by hand:* tack each square of fabric to a paper then oversew together.

This patchwork shape can be used without tacking it to a paper. There is no danger of the pieces being pulled out of shape. The patches must still, however, be cut to size accurately and with the necessary turnings, and with the edges turned under if they are to be oversewn by hand.

Designs with the appearance of stained glass can be made by carefully placing brilliant squares in a grid of patches in softer colours. This, however, should not be confused with what is called Stained Glass Patchwork where the pieces are fitted together as in a jig-saw puzzle and the joins covered with black bias binding.

A cosy made with squares (*figure 10*)

This is simply a rectangle of the size to fit your tea or coffee pot.

Plan your design either in strips, as in diagram 10, or as pictured in figure 10.

When the patchwork is finished remove tackings and papers. Cut a piece of wadding the same size as the finished patchwork and tack it to the back of the patchwork.

Quilt around the squares to hold it all together.

Remove tackings. Line with cotton material. A piping around the edge is a good finish. Rouleau ties of the same material, or ones made from bias binding, are attached to the sides to keep the cosy in place when in use.

If planning to have panels of squares in diagonal lines and plain panels, pay attention to the number of points which you will have at the lower edges. You may find that the corners will not match. Compare diagrams 10 and 11.

Quilting

If your project is more ambitious and you plan to make a bedspread in this manner it will look richer and more professional if you quilt the plain panels. In a large item such as this it is usual to have the plain panels as bands in one piece of material and to hem the coloured strips of patches onto them (*figure 9*).

The quilting could be in diagonal lines which

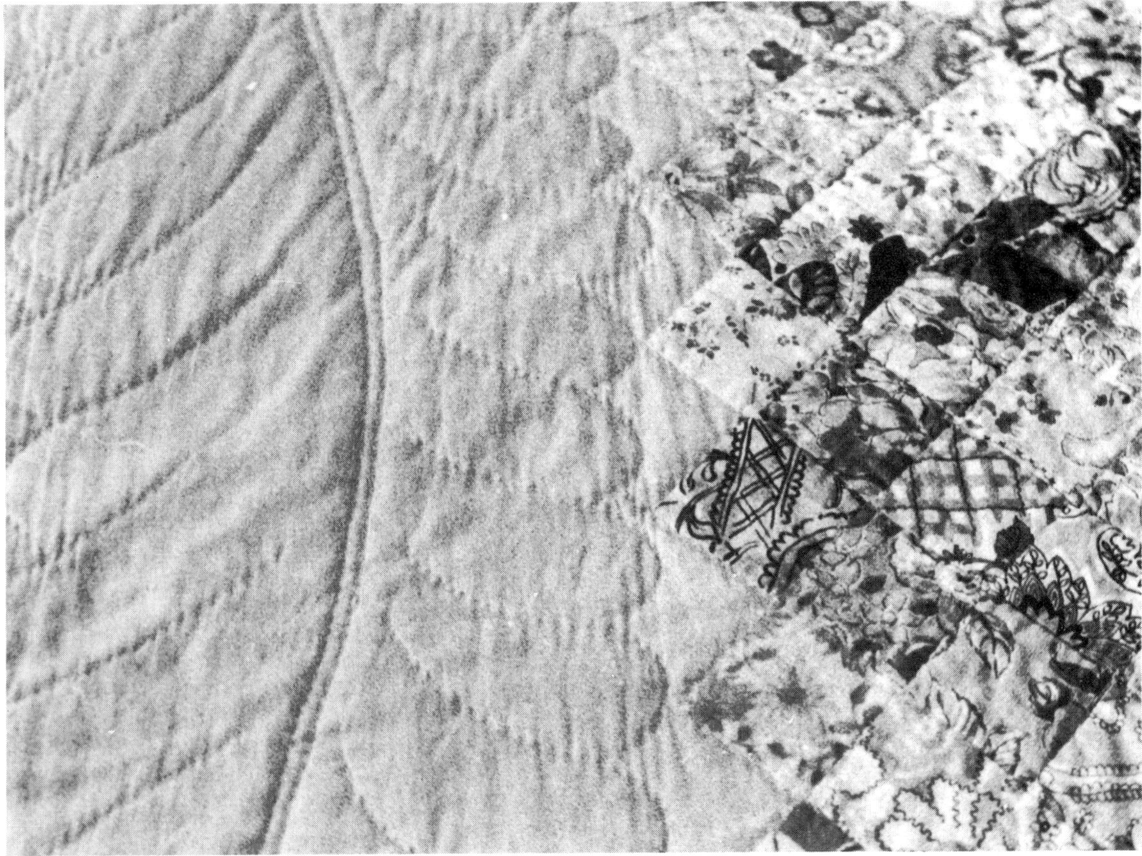

Figure 9 *Detail of bedspread using squares set in diagonal lines with quilted panels.*

follow the lines of the patches or a more decorative one as in figure 9.

Quilting is just running stitch – you will probably find it easier to do if you place your bedspread on a frame and stab your needle up and down. It is the practical, technical way of holding together the patchwork, an interlining of wadding, and the lining. Your needle should penetrate the material at right angles to it – not on a slant.

Some experienced quilters do their stitching as running stitch – not a stabbing-stitch and use a longer needle which becomes quite bowed with use and they find it difficult to get used to a new, straight needle!

It is the regularity and evenness of the stitching, not the extreme smallness of the stitches that marks the quality of quilting.

One square as basic unit

A variation on squared patchwork can be seen in diagram 12. Here the basic unit is one square of a size you choose. All the other rectangular shapes are multiples of that one square.

In some cases you could contrive variety by using a larger shape (e.g. at the top right it could be either nine of the basic squares or one square three times as wide and three times as deep as your basic square). This would obliterate the grid pattern of lines in plain material. However, if it were a floral area this would not be obvious. But in some of the floral areas I have re-arranged the floral pattern to give a different emphasis to the colour and this could not have been done except by keeping the squares in the original size (*figure 11*).

When using differing sizes in this way, calculate carefully the amount needed for turnings.

Figure 10 *Cosy using squares set in diagonal lines.*

Diagram 10 *The correct way of placing squares in diagonal rows to make panels.*

Diagram 11 *Result obtained when an incorrect number of squares is placed in diagonal rows to make panels.*

If an area is in the shape of an L you must make it of small squares or it will have a weakness where the inside corner has no turnings and it would fray and break away with wear.

A design of this kind can be done with a mixture of fabrics but it is also suitable for using dull and shiny materials in a single colour. You can try using just one fabric and cutting certain sections on the grain in one direction and on the opposite grain in others.

Another possibility is to use a furnishing fabric that is a slightly different shade back and front, as in furnishing shantung. With this material pay special attention to the amount for turnings as it frays easily.

The size of your basic square will depend on the size of the article you plan to make and whether one complete section is to be used on its own or whether you intend to make a series of sections and join them. If the latter use is planned then consider how they can be joined to make the best use of the lines and areas produced by juxtaposition.

Squared snuggle quilt (*figure 12*)

Another version of square or rectangular patchwork is to cut two pieces for every patch – a front and a back. Join together around the edges. Leave an opening on one side of each small bag. Stuff each bag with natural fleece or synthetic stuffing. Complete the stitching to close each bag.

Join the bags together. All the bags can be one colour, or one colour on one side and a different colour on the other side, or you can plan a geometric design in more than two colours before commencing the project.

When finished you have a cosy snuggle quilt.

Yet another version of squared patchwork is where square pockets are made with the back of the pocket smaller than the front. For example, with the back 4 in. (10 cm) square and the front $5\frac{1}{2}$ to 6 in. (14 to 16 cm) square. The larger piece is attached to the smaller piece by seaming. Adjust the larger piece to the smaller by making small pleats along the seam line. Leave an opening for stuffing. Join the bags together when stuffed (*figure 12*).

Figure 11 *Sampler using one square as a basic unit.*

Diagram 12 *A design built up using multiples of one unit – in this case a single square.*

For additional warmth, line the quilt with a blanket. Try making the same design using a light-weight material, such as linen, and leaving the pockets unstuffed, for an effective summer quilt.

The diamond

The diamond that can be used with the hexagon is cut from a hexagon. The diamond that can be

Figure 12 *Squared snuggle quilt.*

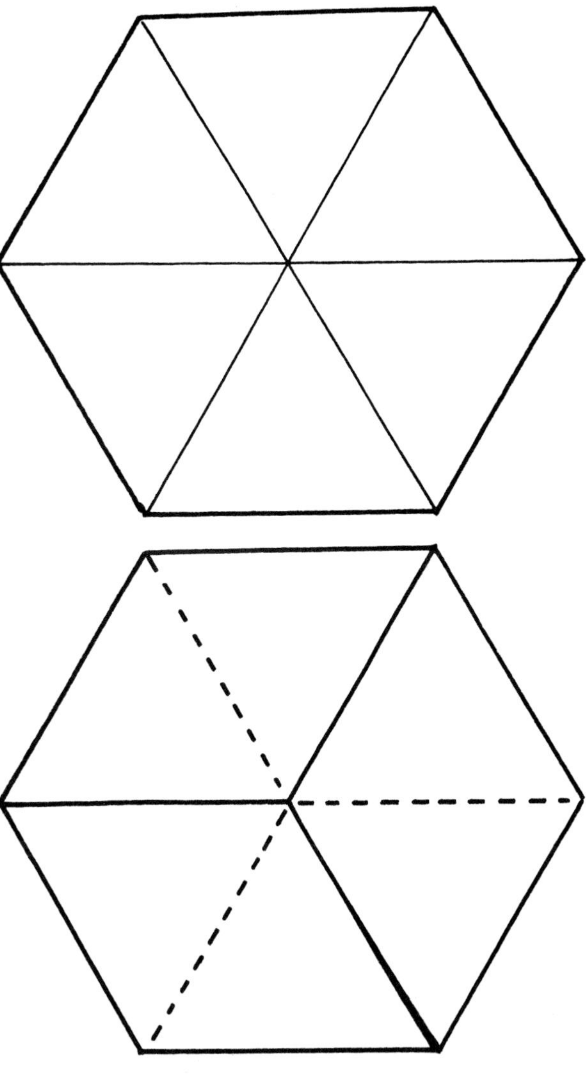

Diagram 13a *and* b *How to obtain diamonds from a hexagon.*

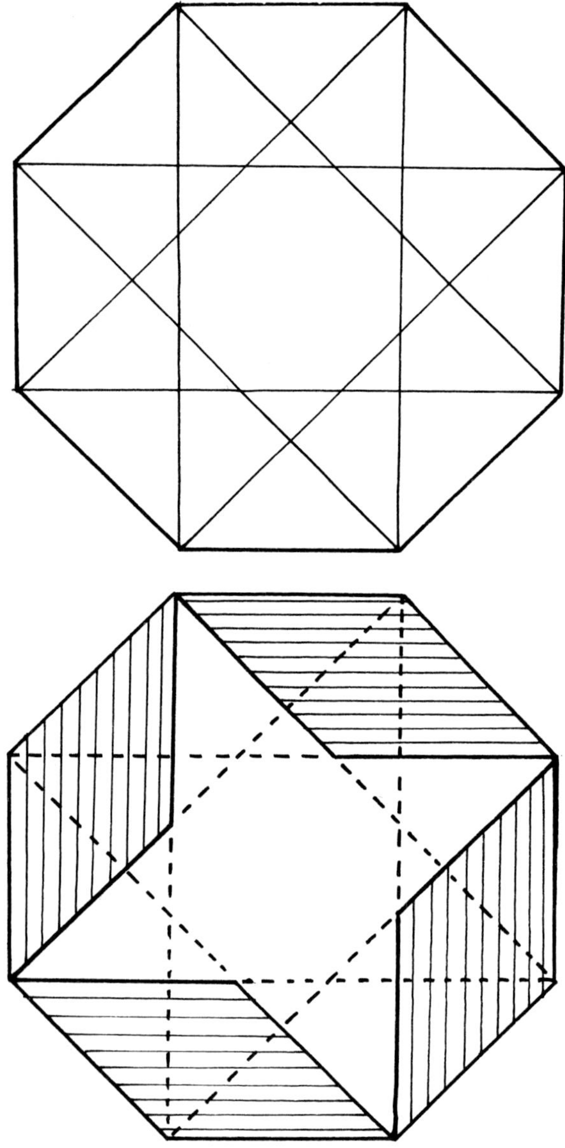

Diagram 14a *and* b *How to obtain diamonds from an octagon.*

used with the octagon is cut from an octagon. They are not the same and cannot be interchanged.

The hexagon diamond

To cut diamonds from a hexagon, draw a hexagon, then connect the corners with lines as in diagram 13a. Each hexagon provides three diamonds (*diagram 13b*).

The octagon diamond

To cut diamonds from an octagon, draw an octagon, then connect the corners as in diagram 14a. Each octagon provides four diamonds, discard the unwanted, white areas (*diagram 14b*).

A hexagon diamond pinwheel (*figure 13*)

Cut six hexagon diamond papers. Cut six half hexagon papers (*diagram 15a*). Cut two 3 in. (7 cm) circles of light-weight cardboard. Cut two circles of wadding the same size as the cardboard. Cut two circles of flannel or other woollen material the same size as above.

Using your circle of cardboard as a template, cut one piece of fabric with turnings. These turnings should be wider than the usual patchwork turnings ($\frac{1}{2}$ to $\frac{3}{4}$ in. [1·25 to 2 cm] is enough).

Cut six fabric diamonds the size of the paper ones plus turnings. Cut six half hexagons the size of the paper ones plus turnings, in fabric contrasting with the diamonds and matching the circle of fabric. Tack fabric to papers.

Join diamonds to make a six-pointed star. These can be joined as two sets of three and then joined across the middle. Whether you work from the outside to the centre each way, or from the centre out each way, is a matter of opinion, but the result is likely to be more satisfactory if it is done in two steps. If you hold your finished star to the light there should not be a hole in the middle.

Join a contrasting half hexagon in each hollow around the outside of the star. Make sure you do not catch the outside turnings into your joining stitches.

When all the half hexagons are joined to the star remove tackings, press the patchwork and make sure that the turnings around the edge are pressed outwards. Remove papers.

On each piece of cardboard stick one piece of wadding – using a minimal amount of glue.

With wadding between patchwork and cardboard, lace the edges of the patchwork from side to side across the back of the cardboard until there are no pleats in the outside edge of the patchwork.

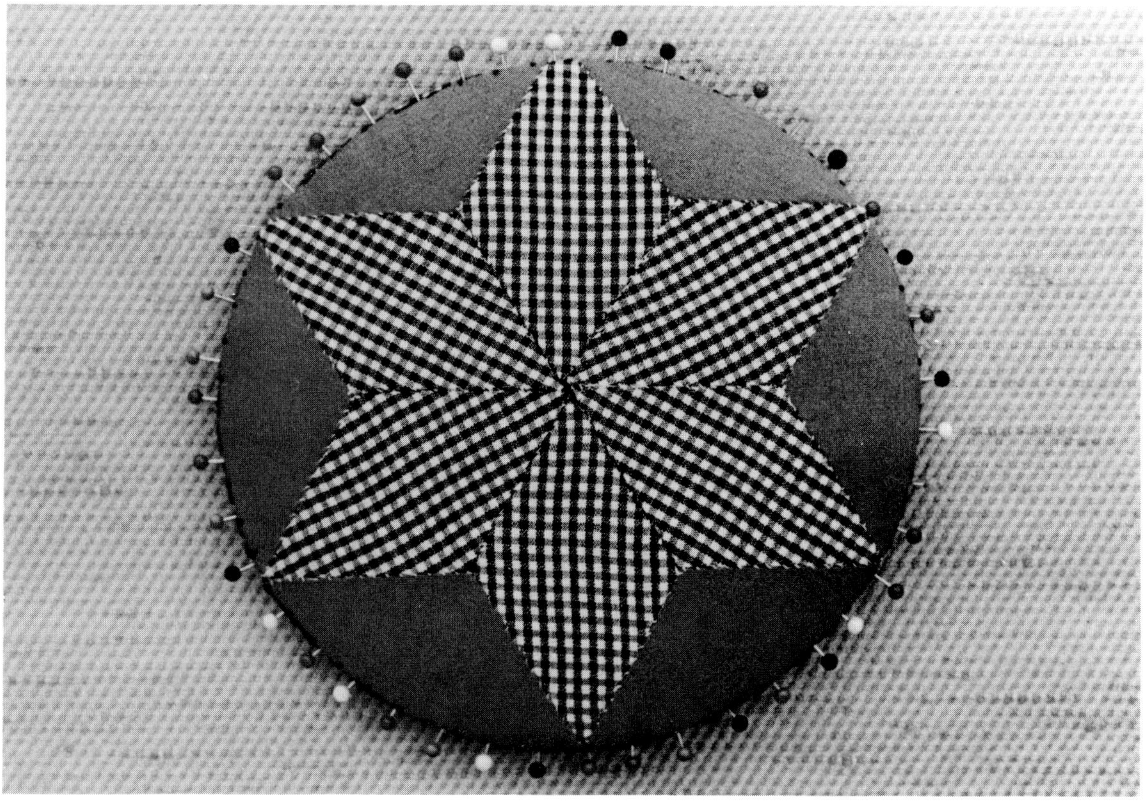

Figure 13 *Diamond pinwheel.*

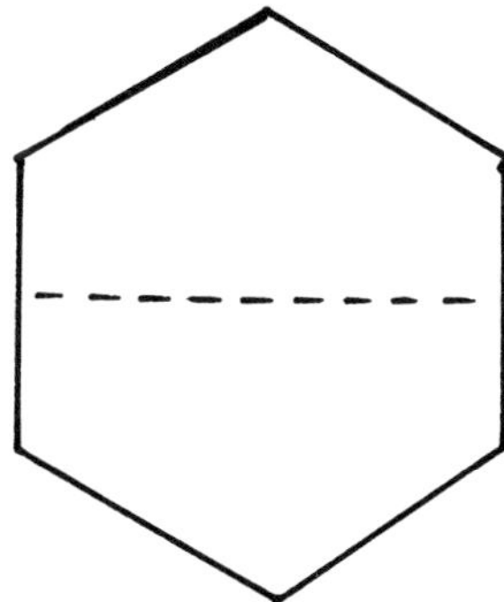

Diagram 15a *How to cut a hexagon to make a half-hexagon. (Cut on dotted line.)*

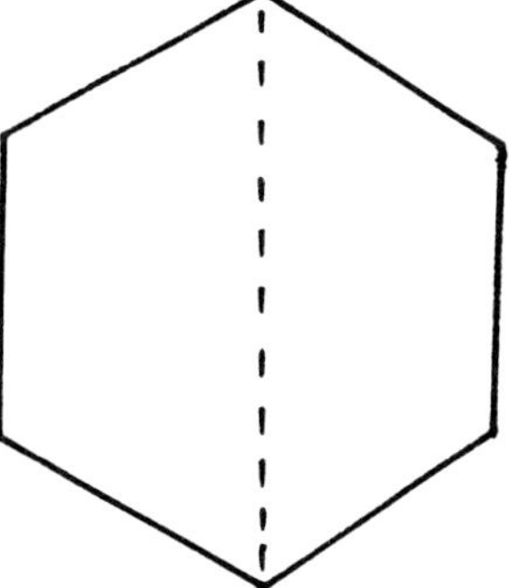

Diagram 15b *Alternative way to cut a hexagon to make a different half-hexagon. (Cut on dotted line.)*

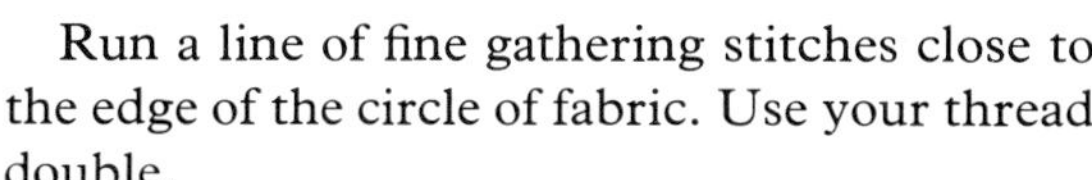

Run a line of fine gathering stitches close to the edge of the circle of fabric. Use your thread double.

Place this material over the padded side of the second piece of cardboard. Draw up the gathering string for a snug fit with evenly spaced gathers. Finish thread securely.

On the inside of both pieces of cardboard glue (in the centre only) a piece of flannel cut to the size of the cardboard. (It must not project beyond the edges of the cardboard.)

Hold both pieces together and join around the edges with a strong ornamental thread. A lacing stitch which goes from side to side, as in

Figure 14 *Bolster cushion using two sizes of diamonds and elongated pentagons. Made by the author.*

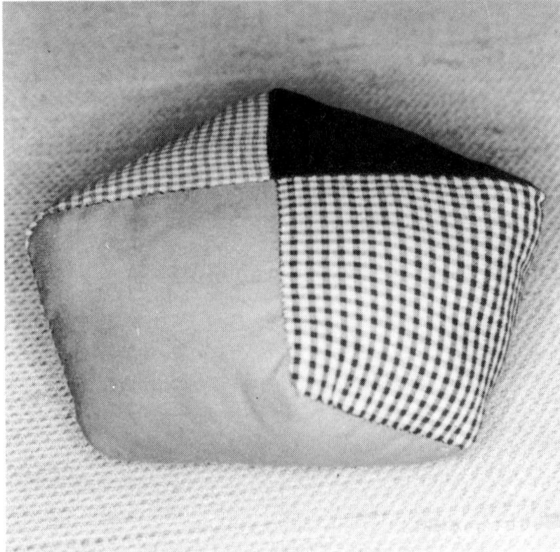

Figure 15 *Oto-dama bag.*

herringbone, is satisfactory.

Your pinwheel is complete when you add a row of coloured glass-headed pins around the edge.

NB There is another half-hexagon (*diagram 15b*). This is used when you are using hexagons and wish to have a straight edge. It fits in quite simply.

The bolster cushion (*figure 14*) is a combination of diamonds in two sizes and elongated pentagons. To make the end and the cylindrical piece fit together, it was necessary to tailor the diamonds around the star and the pairs of triangles (equilateral triangles are half of a hexagon diamond) around the edges of the cylinder so that the edges matched.

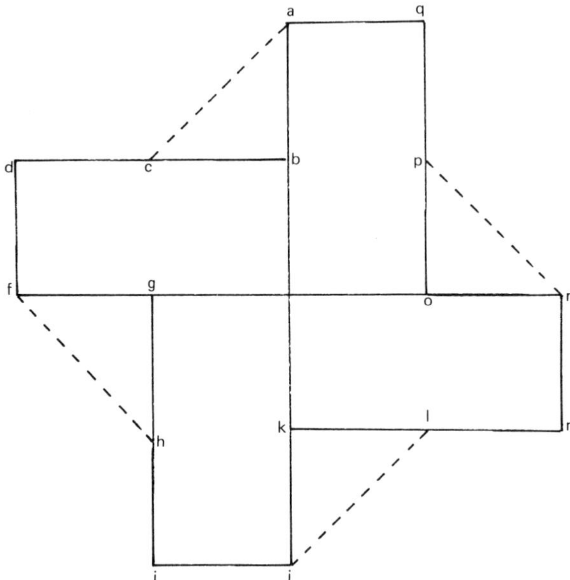

Diagram 16 *How to assemble the pieces of fabric for an Oto-dama bag.*

Figure 16 *Floor cushion.*

The rectangle

Oto-dama bags (*figure 15* and *diagram 16*)

These bags are used in Japan for a game where they toss them to one another. They are the equivalent of an old-fashioned 'bean bag'. They are simply made, but are attractively off-centre and can be used as a pincushion, if desired.

Four strips of material that are twice as long as they are wide, plus ½ in. (1·2 cm) turnings all around are all that are required.

Use a filling suitable to the size and intended use of the bag.

It is easier if the joining of the seams is done in stages.

1 Join **a–b** to **b–c**. Join **f–g** to **g–h**. Join **j–k** to **k–l**. Join **n–o** to **o–p**.

2 Join **c–d** to **a–q**. Join **h–i** to **f–d**. Join **l–m** to **j–i**. Join **p–q** to **n–m**.

Stuff before closing last seam.

Larger-scale patchwork

Floor cushion (*figure 16*)

This floor cushion was made by hand but could easily have been made by machine.

It comprises a panel of furnishing material with square and oblong pieces sewn to it.

Filled with polystyrene pellets, it is light and is comfortable to sit on. It measures 34 in. square (86 cm square).

3 Patchwork using curved outlines

The clamshell

The traditional method of using the clamshells is to place them in parallel rows. Start working from the top and the top of the second row lies neatly over the raw edges of the previous row. Patterns using plain and printed fabrics are usual.

An easier way to assemble the clamshells is to sew them onto a backing. If you draw parallel straight lines across a backing of calico or muslin they should be 1 in. (2·5 cm) apart if you are using the 2 in. (5 cm) template. These provide useful guide lines. (Faded or washed-out gingham with checks of this size can be used provided the checks will not show through the surface material.)

Make a piece of patchwork as large as you require for your project and when finished use it as a piece of fabric and cut to your requirements.

The circular example (*figure 17*) was made using larger clamshells for the outer ring and smaller ones for the inner ring. The clamshells in the intervening row were drawn with a compass, radius $1\frac{1}{4}$ in. (3·2 cm).

The clamshells can be assembled in other ways. See what you can achieve.

The clamshell is derived from circles as in diagram 17. It is usual to buy 2 in. and 3 in. (5 cm and 7·5 cm) templates, but it is also possible to make your own.

Cutting templates

This is a workable method. For the 2 in. (5 cm) size:

Draw three parallel horizontal lines 1 in. (2·5 cm) apart and crossed at $2\frac{1}{2}$ in. (6·25 cm) intervals by lines.

With the radius of your compass 1 in. (2·5 cm) and centred on the middle line, midway at **'c'** in each division, draw a series of circles. There will be $\frac{1}{2}$ in. (1 cm) between them.

Set the point of your compass on the bottom line where the perpendicular cuts it at **'d'**.

Diagram 17 *How to obtain the clamshell shapes.*

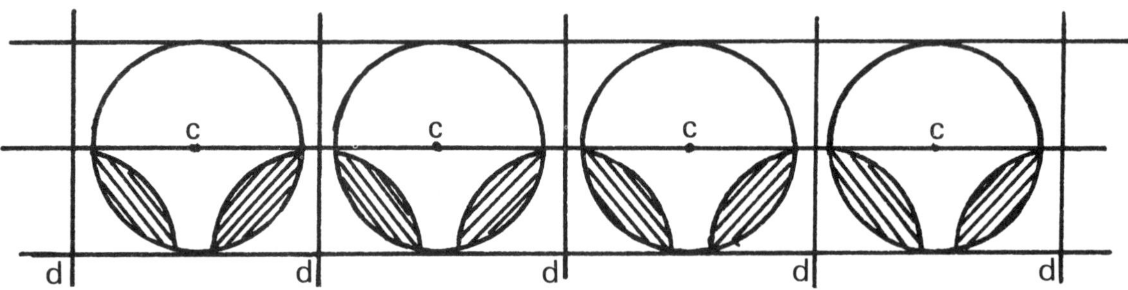

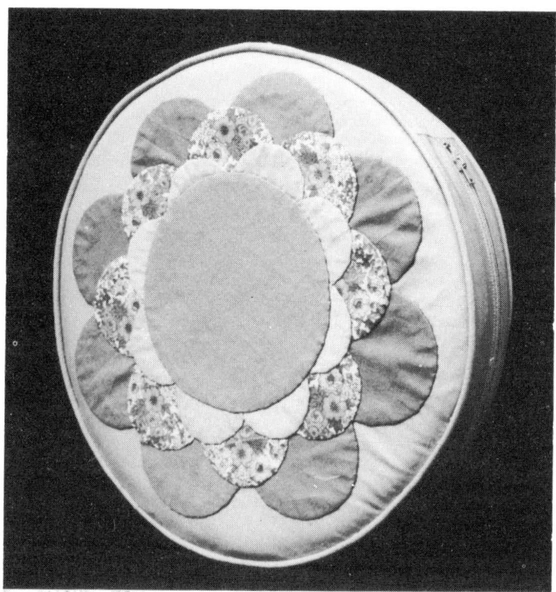

Figure 17 *Clamshells set in circles; an example of a cushion with a wall.*

With the compass still set at 1 in. (2·5 cm) radius draw arcs of this circle where they cut the two adjacent circles. Repeat with the other circles.

Cut out the circles and discard the shaded parts (*diagram 17*).

For the 3 in. (7·25 cm) size all your requirements will be half as big again.

Method of working

Cut as many papers as you need. Cut the same number of pieces of fabric with the usual amount of turnings all around. *The papers are only used as a guide for the shape of the patches.* They are not stitched to the patches in the usual manner. Pin a paper to each patch.

Make tiny pleats in the fabric and stitch in place as you turn the seam allowance over so that you can adjust the *outer* edge of the patch to the shape of the curve of the paper.

Do not let your stitching go through the paper.

Pin patches in place with the tiny straight edge at the base resting on one of the lines which you have drawn on the backing.

Slip stitch *folded* edge of first row of patches onto backing – side by side with edges touching only at their widest part.

Remove pins from this row of patches and *take out the papers.*

Pin and sew second row of patches over the raw edges of the previous row. Overlap should be about $\frac{1}{4}$ in. (6 mm). The straight edges should be resting on the next row down and the clamshells just touching, as previously (*diagram 18*).

Continue in this manner until area is filled (*figure 18*).

Drunkard's Path

To make this pattern you start with a basic square and add a quadrant (quarter circle) of different coloured fabric and then arrange a number of squares in different groupings so that the quadrant makes solid or wandering patterns.

Counterchange patterns – i.e. reversing the combinations of colour in some places – were frequent in this method.

1 Cut quadrant papers the size you wish and then cut fabric to match with $\frac{1}{4}$ in. (6 mm) turnings on the curved edge.

Pin paper to fabric and turn curved edge over paper in the same way as described for clamshells and in figure 19.

Stitch quadrant onto one corner of square of fabric. Remove paper. Or:

2 Draw the quadrant and square on paper (*diagram 19*). Cut out quadrant.

Cut fabric square, minus quadrant, but with usual amount for seam allowance on curved edge.

Cut quadrant in fabric with allowance for turning on curved edge.

If you are familiar with dressmaking techniques and are used to setting in a sleeve you will have no difficulty joining these two pieces together.

Pin at either end, in the centre and in between with the right sides facing. Using your thumb to hold the convex edge onto the concave edge, seam with a fine stitch. Small snips around the convex edge will help the material to sit flat.

When complete, iron on the right side and it should sit quite flat. Join the finished squares into the desired pattern.

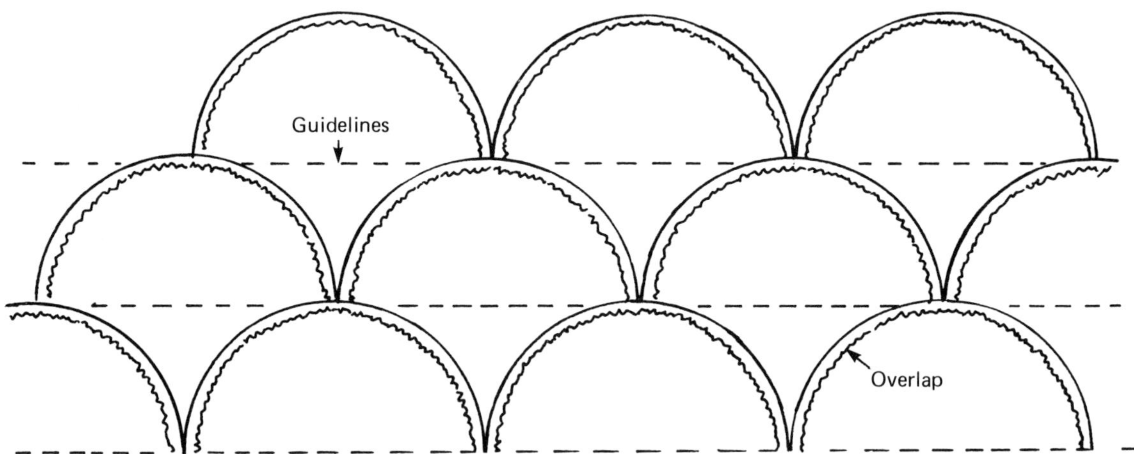

Diagram 18 *How to place the clamshell shapes in horizontal lines.*

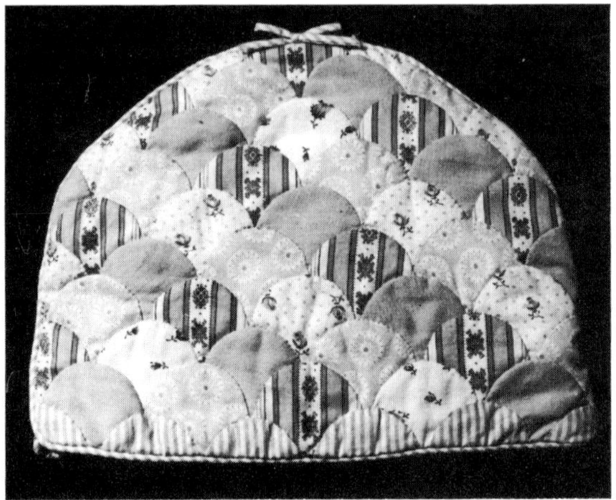

Figure 18 *Cosy using clamshells set in straight rows.*

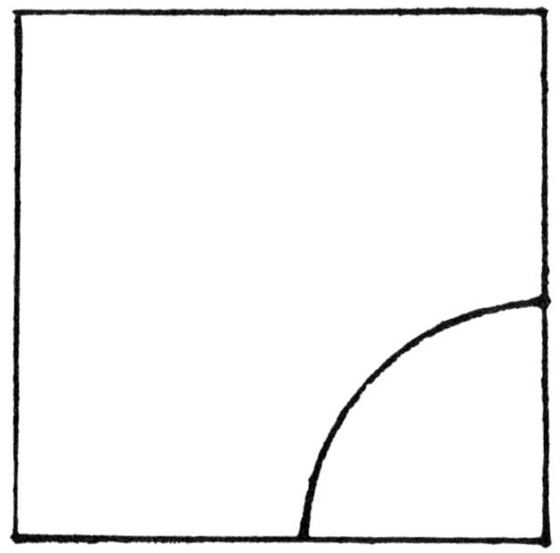

Diagram 19 *How to place the quarter-circle pieces on the squares in patterns such as Drunkard's Path.*

For a thorough and interesting analysis of the ways in which this block can be used I refer readers to Margaret Ickis, *The Standard Book of Quilt Making and Collecting*, Dover, 1959 (pp. 74–7).

Dresden Plate

To make a template for this design draw a circle 10–12 in. (25·5–30·5 cm) in diameter on paper. Cut it out carefully and fold it in half, then in half again. With these four quadrants fold again and again into segments to obtain as many divisions as you wish. Between 12 and 24 segments are usual in this design. The number of segments in each plate should be constant throughout the article.

A circle about 3–4 in. (7·5–10 cm) in diameter in plain colour is placed in the centre of the Dresden Plate. All pieces surrounding the plain centre should be small patterned fabrics so that the effect is a colourful blur of pattern. Scallop the edges of the 'plate' and apply to a plain background square.

The example in figure 20 is a slight variant to the usual Dresden Plate. It has pointed corners and detail in the centre. It is unusual, also, in that it is strong colours, mainly reds and golds, and on a black square it is very striking.

Cut as many plates as required in paper and, with turnings, in fabric. If you are making this design by machine you do not need to tack the fabric to papers. Otherwise tack the fabric to papers as usual. I find the seams are more evenly

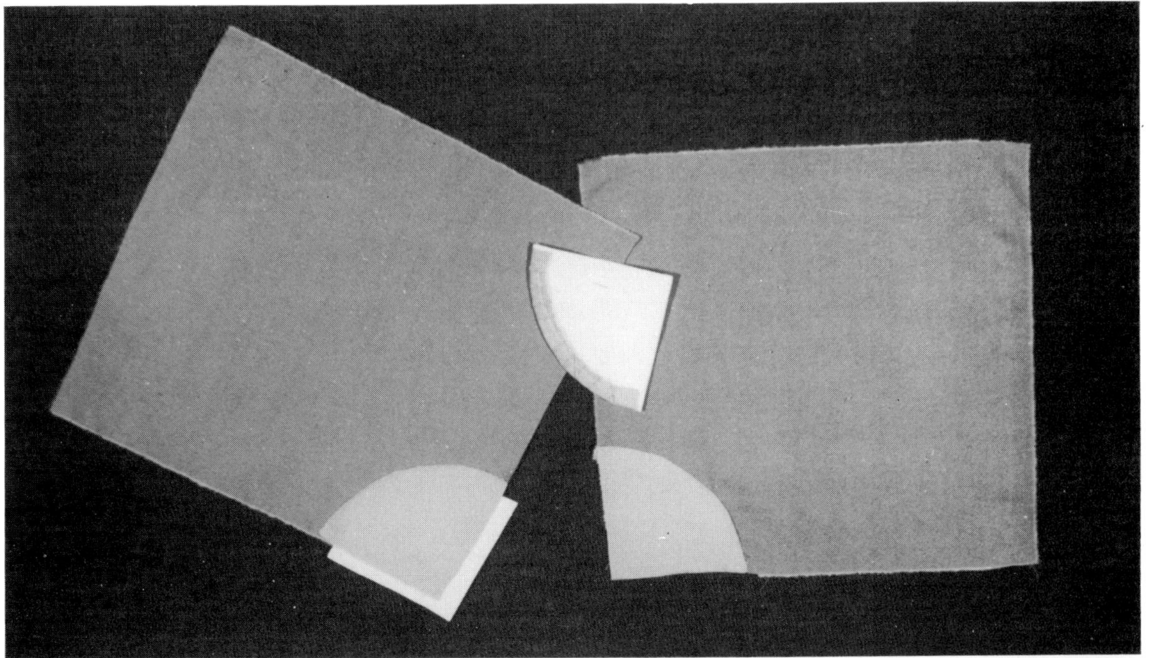

Figure 19 *Shows quarter circle of fabric with curved edge pleated to fit.* Left: *patch has been applied and paper shape is being removed.* Right: *the curved edge has been seamed to the patch.*

and firmly sewn if they are done in this way rather than joined with running stitch. The part beneath the central circle can be cut away.

A quilt can be made of squares with a plate on each, or alternate the squares with plain ones of the same size. The colour of the squares may be of the same colour as the circle in the centre or a contrasting colour.

The idea of making squares with an applied design and then joining them is the basis of much contemporary American patchwork.

If just one quarter of the segments is joined and a quarter circle of dark fabric is used in the point, the pattern is called 'Grandmother's Fan'.

The points of the fan can be cut away beneath the dark area.

This is, also, applied to a plain background.

If the quarters are placed in an alternate up and down grouping with the points scooped off, you achieve a wavy rope that is then applied to a plain background (*figure 21*).

Figure 20 *Dresden Plate sampler with unusual details.*

Segmented ball (*figure 22*)

For this you must cut your own papers as there are no templates and the shapes are easily derived. You need a compass, a ruler and paper.

Draw three squares. For a first attempt do not

Figure 21 *Wavy Rope cushion.*

have the sides of the squares less than 2 in. (5 cm) (*diagram 20a, 20b, 20c*).

To cut the papers

Diagram a Set the compass on a 2 in. (5 cm) radius. Using **c** as the centre point draw an arc from **a** to **b**.

Diagram b Repeat instructions for diagram 20a.

Diagram c Repeat again. Then move the compass point to D and draw an arc from **a** to **b**.

Cut out the quadrants A and B and the oval C and discard shaded areas.

To assemble the parts

Cut fabric to fit paper shapes. Turnings must be small but adequate to prevent fraying. Tack to papers, turning edges over on all sides.

Each segment requires a set of the papers A, B and C. There are 12 segments so you need 36 papers in all – 12 oval ones and 24 quadrants.

Choose a wide variety of fabrics and patterns of light weight.

Sew two quadrants together along straight sides, right sides facing but leave a small gap in the middle of one side. Sew an oval between the two curved edges. Remove papers. Turn inside out and stuff firmly. Stitch gap (*figure 22*).

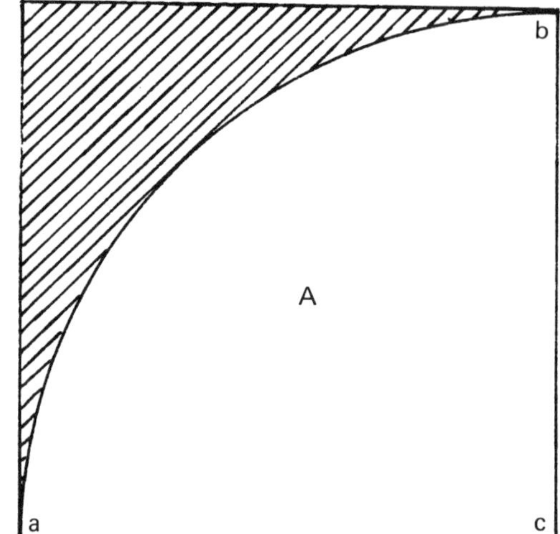

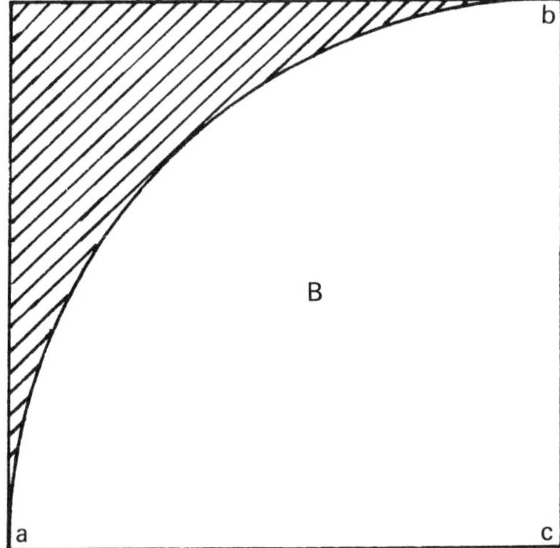

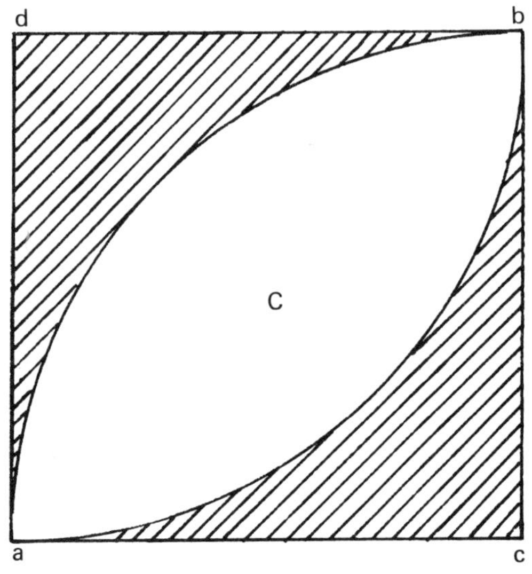

Diagram 20 *Plans to show the shapes necessary to make the sections of the segmented ball. (Discard shaded areas.)*

Figure 22 *Segmented balls and two individual segments. Top right-hand ball and segments are made in 2 in. (5 cm) size.*

To assemble the segments

1 Place four segments in a circle. Sew firmly together in the centre where the points meet and at outside points where they touch. Do this with strong, toning, coloured thread.

2 Place four more segments in a similar arrangement but do not sew the points together in the centre. Sew outside points together in three places only.

3 Wrap the second group of four around the previous group. Push points firmly into previous centre and join the outside edge firmly.

4 Place remaining four segments together as in paragraph 2. Join outside points in three places. Wrap around previous eight in a direction which is different to both the other groups. Join firmly. You will probably need to push the points together with quite a lot of pressure.

Very small segmented balls make delightful pincushions but are *very* fiddly to make. As a child's toy these are good as small hands can hold just one segment.

Suffolk Puffs

No templates or papers are required for this variety of patchwork. The material needs to be light and soft. Lingerie fabrics and polyester georgettes are ideal.

Cut your fabric in circles. Use a plate, a saucer or similar object to get your size and draw around it. Cut the circles out. Stitch a gather-string while turning a small hem, and then pull up as tight as possible and finish the thread securely. Use the thread double so that it will not break when pulled tightly (*figure 23*).

When you have made as many 'puffs' as you need assemble them by catching together. Assemble in straight rows, either as in diagram 21a or in diagram 21b.

Do not press this variety of patchwork as this flattens the essential quality of the puffs.

If making a bedspread it is important that the

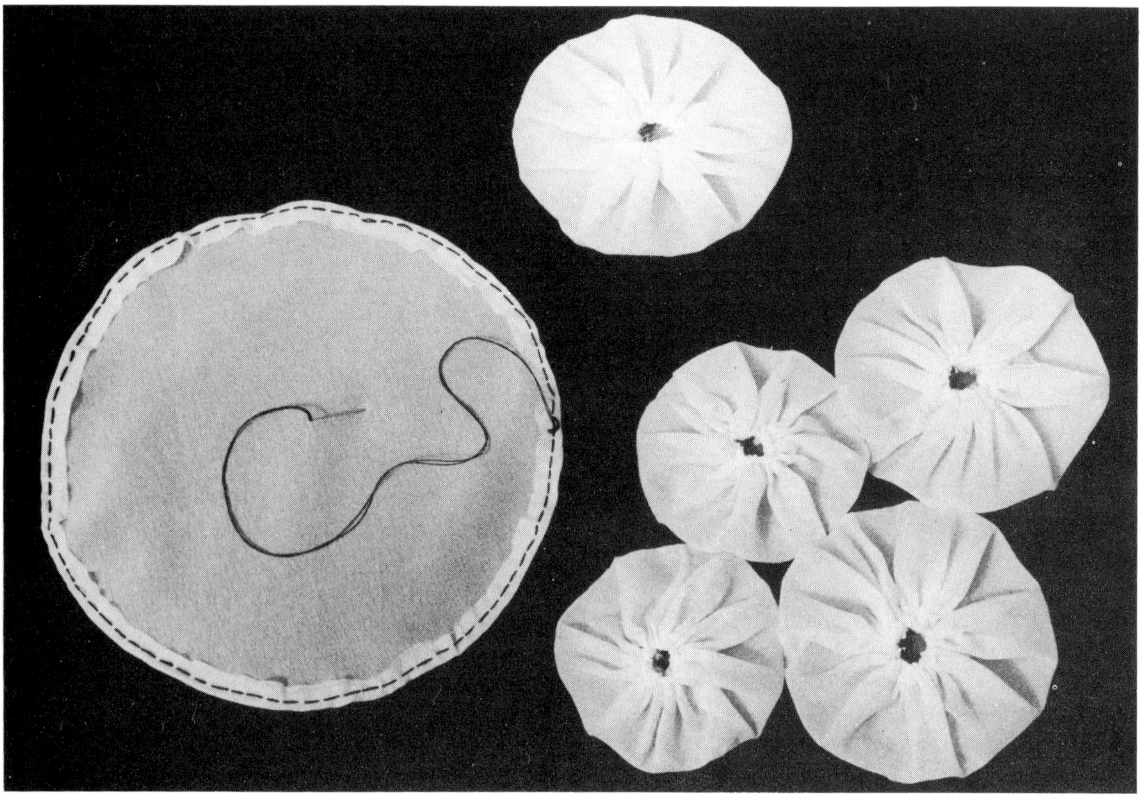

Figure 23 *Suffolk Puffs.*

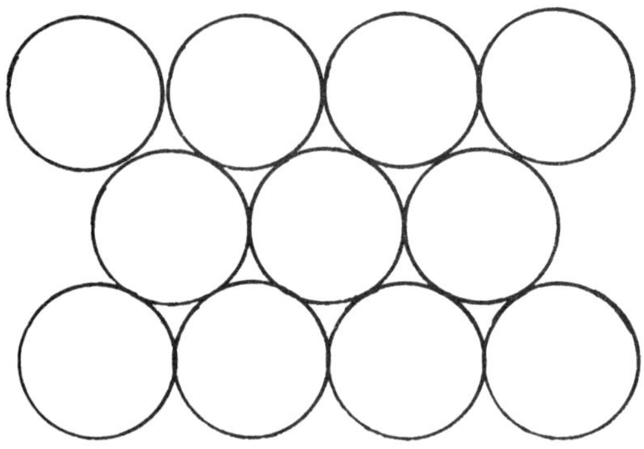

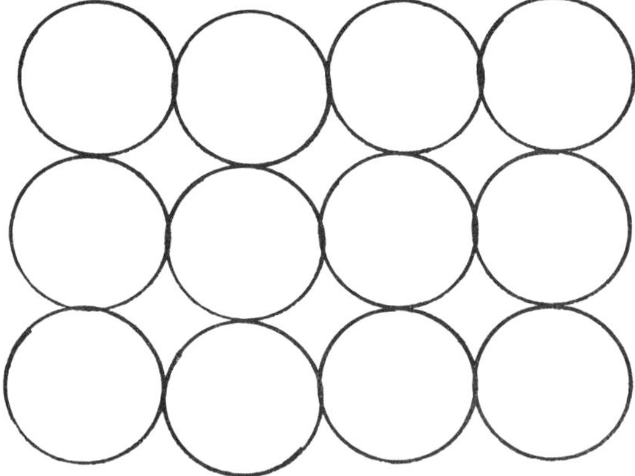

Diagram 21 *Plans to show two different ways of joining Suffolk Puffs.*

fabrics used should be light-weight and easy to wash. Lingerie fabrics are ideal, but a material such as poplin would be too heavy and take too long to dry.

Boudoir glamour (*figure 24*)

There has been so much nostalgic interest in the fashions of the 'twenties and 'thirties that I feel this must be the title of figure 24. The five rows of puffs increase in size and the materials vary.

Row 1 There are 12 puffs, $4\frac{1}{2}$ in. (11·25 cm) diameter in very fine lawn – white with a pink flower.

Row 2 There are 13 puffs, $5\frac{1}{2}$ in. (13·75 cm) diameter in white polyester georgette.

Row 3 There are 14 puffs, 7 in. (17·5 cm) diameter in white polyester georgette with a pink flower bonded to the georgette in the centre of the circle.

Figure 24 *Boudoir glamour.*

Row 4 There are 11 puffs, 9 in. (22·5 cm) and 2 puffs, 7 in. (17·5 cm) diameter in pink polyester georgette.

Row 5 There are 14 puffs, 11 in. (27·5 cm) diameter in pink polyester georgette.

For Row 3 cut a small circle of material containing a flower from the patterned material and bond it (*see p. 98*) to the centre of the circle of fabric before inserting the gather-string in the outside edge. When the gather-string is drawn up the flower should be seen through the hole.

It would be useless to do this in a puff smaller in size than this because the gathers pull closer together and there would be no hole to see through.

Be careful to cut a tidy shape for the flower piece because if you are using a transparent fabric for the puffs the bonded shape will be visible from the back of the puff. Some years ago a student made a basinette quilt and on the back of every puff was a teddy bear!

In Row 4 there is a smaller puff at each end of the row.

In Row 5 the puff at each end of the row is sewn to the end puff in both Row 4 and Row 3. This gives a curve to the lower edge of the cape.

The ties can be of the georgette or ribbon.

4 Special effects using shape and colour

Making the most of fabrics

Many of the basic shapes so far discussed can be used in conjunction with clever colour combinations to achieve striking effects. Figure 25 shows a simple but effective use of shape and colour. Patchwork gives you the opportunity to play around with shape and colour and often the material itself will suggest ideas. In figure 26 the arrangement of the central shapes cleverly changes sizes to make the best use of the design on this fabric. Note the introduction of half hexagons which are set in an unusual manner to achieve this.

Figure 27 shows a miniature cot quilt making clever use of the tiny strawberry pattern. It uses $\frac{1}{4}$ in. (6 mm) hexagons and derivatives – elongated pentagons, half hexagons and diamonds.

Working with stripes

A striped fabric can also be used to great effect in patchwork. The elongated pentagon particularly lends itself to this design because, if the stripes are cut in such a way as to make concentric lines, it is possible to have these lines right into the centre. Figure 28 has been cut in such a way. A casual look might suggest it is a hexagon surrounded by hexagons, but this is not correct.

I do not recommend that you tackle a complicated design using stripes for your first project. The one in figure 29 looks simple enough in diagram 22. (*See p. 12* in Chapter 1 which talks about cutting on the grain of the fabric.) In this case the template is placed with the grain running through the longest measurement from point to point of the church windows. The church windows are then angled against each other which means that the centre cross is on the bias but elsewhere the grain runs horizontally and vertically. It is imperative in a case such as this for you to know where the lines of the fabric will join up and cut accordingly.

This particular piece of fabric was quite a cheap black cotton printed with gold stripes but the printed lines ran absolutely true. It is usually better to use material with a woven stripe for this kind of exercise.

Optical illusion patchwork

Child's Blocks

This pattern makes use of hexagon diamonds. Each block is made up of three diamonds and as long as the sequence of colour is always the same (e.g. the darkest one is always the same one of the two vertical positions), it presents no problems.

The three diamonds can be three different colours or some plain and some patterned – it is the relative strength of the tones that does matter.

When cutting your patches make sure that the grain of the material runs across the top diamond and the side ones have the grain running from top to bottom (*diagram 23*).

Figure 25 *Draughts board and bag. Made in black and white cotton fabrics, it rolls up for easy storage. A simple, but effective use of colour.*

Figure 26 *Manipulating shapes; detail of a cot quilt which cleverly adapts the design on this fabric to best advantage.*

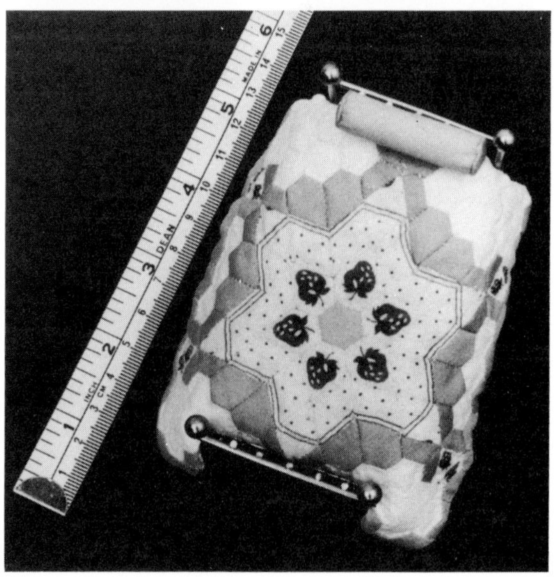

Figure 27 *A miniature quilt using* $\frac{1}{4}$ *in. (6 mm) hexagons and derivatives.*

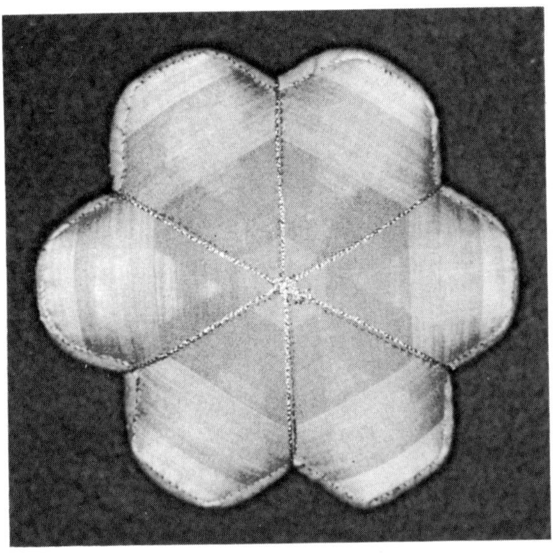

Figure 28 *Elongated pentagon pincushion. The shape of the pieces enables the pattern of stripes to continue right into the centre.*

Figure 29 *Striped mini cushion. (Size: 6½ in. [16·25 cm] square).*

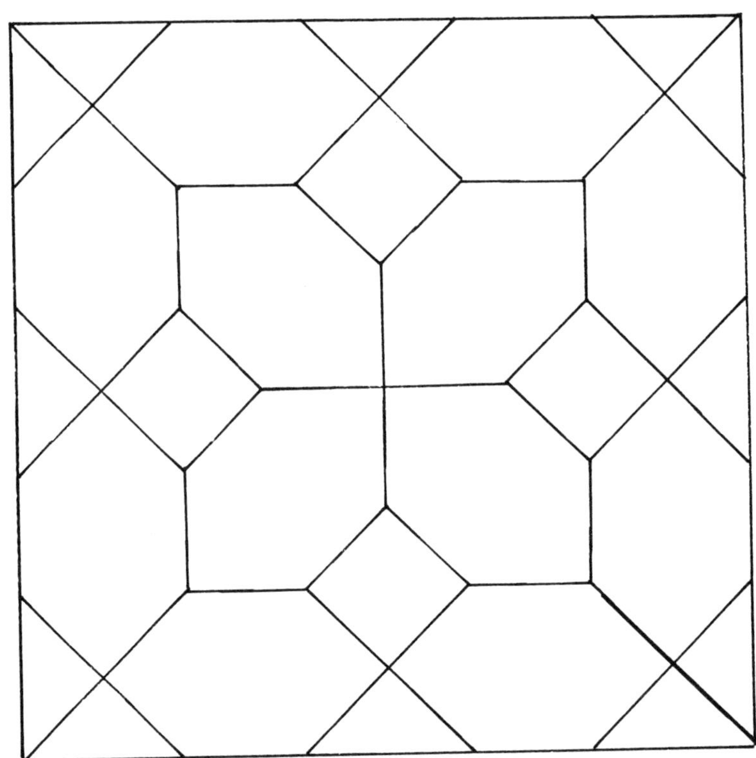

Diagram 22 *The plan for the striped mini-cushion illustrated in* figure 29. *The cutting of the pieces must be carefully worked out to make use of the pattern created by the stripes.*

Figure 30 *Unfinished quilt from the nineteenth century, where light/dark areas in diamonds are not consistent. The effect is quite dazzling.* From the Embroiderers' Guild Collection.

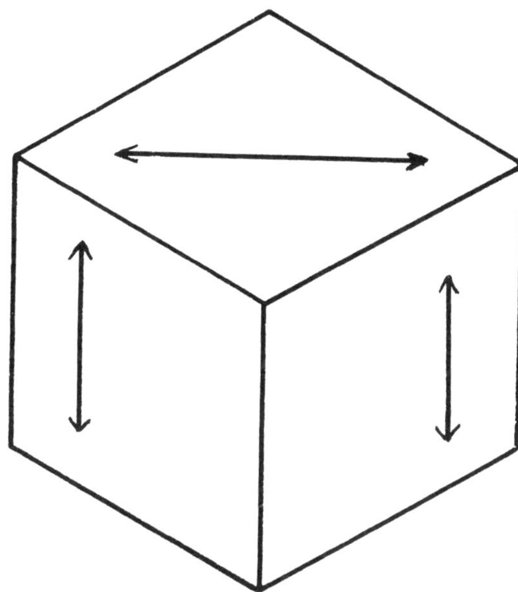

Diagram 23 *Arrows show the way the fabric grain should run for Child's Blocks pattern.*

The blocks can cover the whole area as in figure 30 or be arranged so that there are areas of blocks and plain areas as well. These plain areas can be the hexagon of the size from which the diamonds were cut (*figure 31*).

The pleated pattern which is on two sides of the cushion in figure 32 cannot be used on all sides as it does not fit into the hexagon from all angles. Two sides are plain like the background.

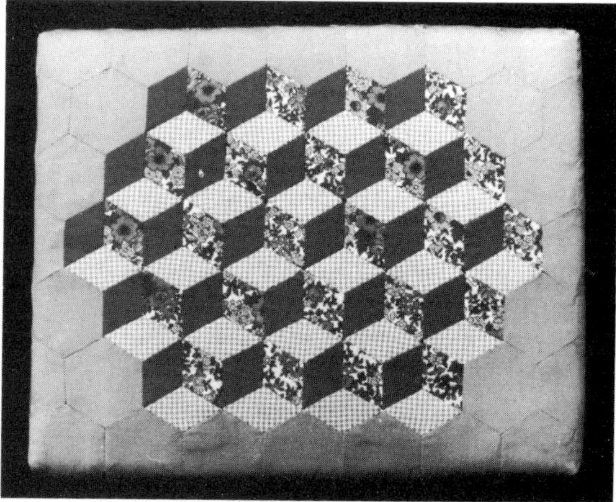

Figure 31 *Cushion with 'Child's Blocks' pattern medallion.*

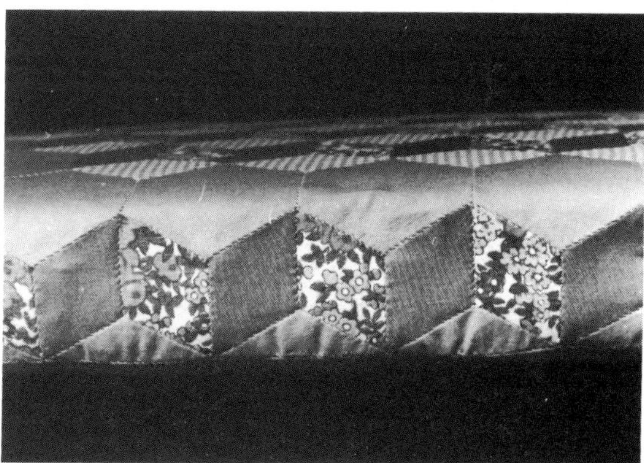

Figure 32 *'Pleated' pattern on wall of cushion in* figure 31.

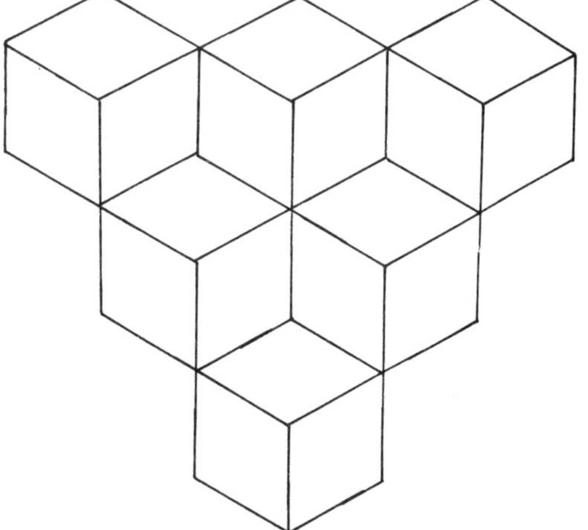

Diagram 24 *How to arrange hexagon diamonds to make the Child's Blocks.*

Figure 33 *Doll's dress. An English piece of patchwork with silk embroidery dating back to 1865. Presented by Lady Nicholson and her daughter.* Reproduced by permission of the National Gallery of Victoria, Melbourne, Australia.

This cushion has the patchwork carried over the sides and is shaped at the corners to fit the foam insert. The back of the cushion can either be plain material or patchwork to match the front.

A cushion pad should measure $\frac{1}{2}$–1 in. (1·25–2·5 cm) larger than the finished cushion. For further details regarding finishing cushions *see pages 96 and 98*.

Figure 33 shows Child's Blocks incorporated into a doll's dress. This would also fit a child of two to three years. Figures 34, 35a and 35b and the back jacket show further examples of optical illusion patchwork.

Crazy patchwork

Unlike the previous forms of patchwork, crazy patchwork requires no templates and little or no planning, unless a definite colour scheme is to be followed. The effect is achieved by the random juxtaposition of shape and colour.

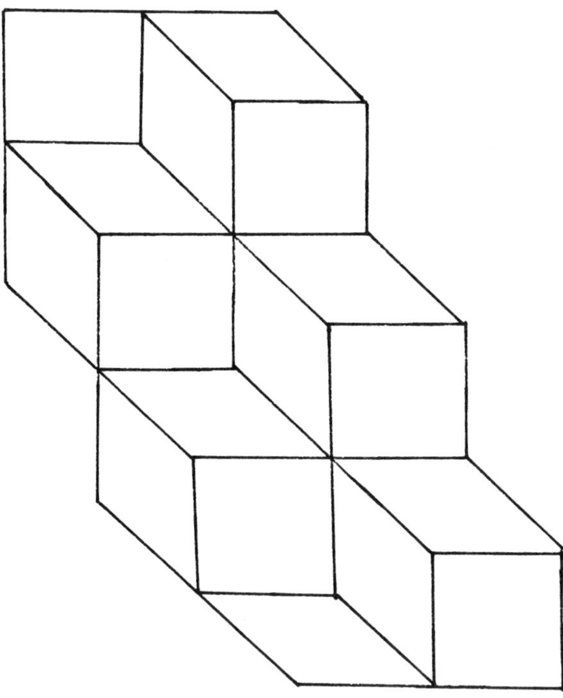

Diagram 25 *How to arrange squares and octagon diamonds to make the Steps and Stairs pattern shown in* figure 34.

Figure 34 *An optical illusion sampler using squares and octagon diamonds.*

Figure 35a *Optical illusion panel using a simple piece of black and white patchwork which is set in the base of a black box.*

Figure 35b *The front of the box in* 35a *is ribbed glass which gives this effect.*

This form was a great favourite in Victorian times. It uses pieces of any weight material and needs a backing of calico or other cotton fabric.

Here, the odd shapes of scraps of material are used to their advantage and all are placed overlapping each other to make a veritable kaleidoscope of colour. The patches are often

Figure 36a *and* b *Detail of a crazy patchwork quilt in the collection of Worthing Museum where practically every piece has added embroidery.*

embroidered, as in figures 36a and 36b. Any fabrics – even metallic ones – can be used in this colourful array, unless the article is to be washable when the character of the materials must play a part in the selection. Quite small items can use very small scraps. When innoculated with the patchwork 'bug' the enthusiast never discards anything!

My example of a bedspread is on a dolls' house size bed so to keep it in scale the pieces are minute. The problem here was to scale the stitching to comparable size (*figure 37*).

When you are satisfied that the pieces are arranged to their best advantage pin and then tack the pieces in place. Cover the raw edges of the pieces with herringbone or feather stitching. You do not turn the edges under. A neutral colour is best for the stitching. Many a Victorian piece was sewn in black or other dark colour.

Do experiment with small pieces of very vivid colour amongst more sombre ones. A small piece of bright turquoise blue or vivid green can 'lift' a whole cushion.

1 *'Palm Frond'. The maker here experiments with straight line sewing (machining) to get away from the strictly geometric to achieve a more natural visual effect.*

2 *'Palm Frond' detail.*

3 *'After Christmas' by Barbara Macey. The first in a series of wall quilts exploring the uses of the quarter circle block. Fabrics used were cottons, synthetic satins and taffetas. The red fabrics are grouped to define faint fish-scale shapes within the overlapping 'baubles'.*

4 *'After Christmas' detail.*

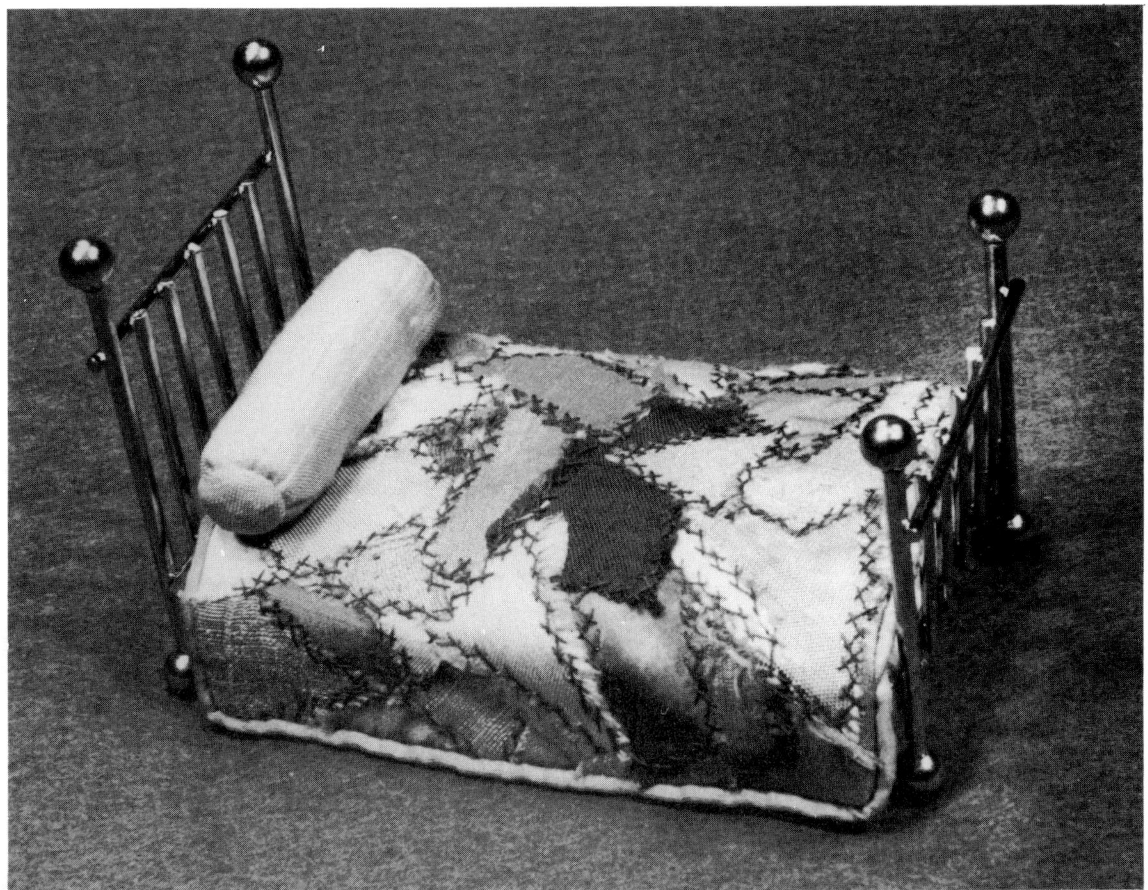

Figure 37 *Quilt made for a doll's bed in crazy patchwork.*

The purpose for which you intend your crazy patchwork will determine how it should be finished. Later sections of this book will deal with a number of ways of finishing work. It could be made into a bag, used as the top of a box, finished as a cushion or hung on a wall. The possibilities are endless.

5 Folded patchwork

Cathedral Window patchwork

This variety of patchwork was introduced comparatively recently – it has only been in use for about 100 years. Its advantage is that, when completed, there is no lining or interlining to be done.

Its disadvantage, in my opinion, is the amount of material it uses. Except for the gaily coloured windows it is impossible to use scraps as the main part of the patches. In the case of a quilt this is a very considerable amount of fabric. You must keep the ground material as light in weight as possible or the finished quilt will be very heavy. Muslin or lawn are usual.

Every teacher who uses this variety of patchwork has her own way of doing it. These instructions may appear fiddly but if you follow step-by-step it all works out and having done it once there is no further trouble.

Most of the quilts that I have seen have had a very pale colour for the background – frequently white – and all the windows have been very gay but recently I saw one with a beige background and all the windows in muted brown tones – it was attractive and unusual.

Do not press the work at any stage after you start sewing – it will flatten the pieces too much.

Pincushion (*figure 38*)

1 Cut a 4 in. (10 cm) square template in light cardboard.

2 Using your background material, cut or tear it into strips of equal width. For my sample pincushion I use 5 in. (12·5 cm) wide strips. The strips must be on the grain of the material. (If torn, they must be, as you cannot tear fabric on the bias.)

3 Cut these strips to make 5 in. (12·5 cm) squares.

4 Your squares must be exactly square and exactly the same size.

5 Place the cardboard template on top of a piece of material. There will be $\frac{1}{2}$ in. (1·2 cm) material around the edge of the template. Press this edge over the cardboard template. Do this on all sides of all the pieces of material. Your squares of material should now measure 4 in. (10 cm) (*diagram 26i*).

6 Mark the centre point on each side of each square.

7 Take a square and fold **a** to **b** and **c** to **d** (*diagram 26ii*).

8 Oversew the edges taking only the minimal amount of fabric in the stitching. Commence to sew at the fold and stop halfway along the side. Repeat on other side of patch.

9 Re-fold the patch taking **a** to **c** and **b** to **d**. Stitch as previously. These stitches will not be seen but stitch with matching thread, if possible.

10 Smooth this patch, making sure the seams lie flat. The four original corners should now touch at the centre (*diagram 26iii*).

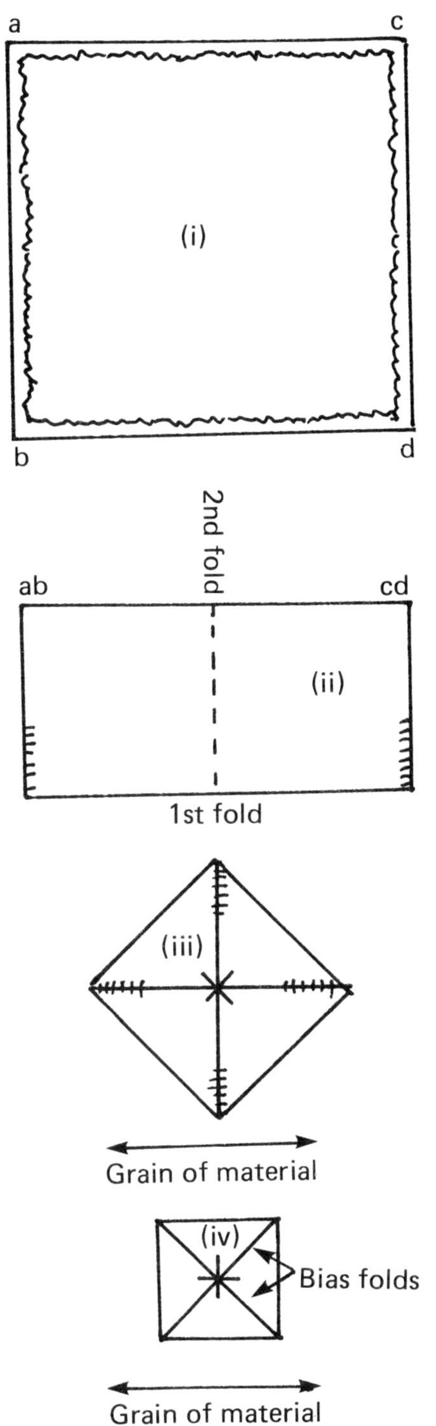

Diagram 26 *How to fold a square of fabric to make one Cathedral patchwork piece and to join it to similar pieces.*

11 Join the points securely with crossing stitches but do not allow the stitches to show on the back of the patch.

12 Again bring the four corners to the centre and stitch together. (No seams at the side, this time.) Leave this piece on one side (*diagram 26iv*).

13 Make three more patches in exactly the same way. (Follow steps 7–12.)

14 Join the four patches together to make a square. Stitch seams by oversewing, smooth sides facing (*diagram 27*).

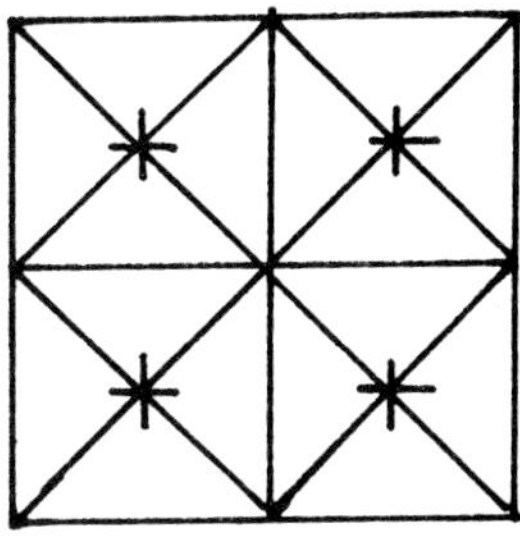

Diagram 27 *Four squares of Cathedral patchwork joined together.*

15 Notice that the unattached, diagonal folds are on the bias and will roll.

16 Cut a small square of patterned material which just fits inside each of the squares bounded by the bias fold. Pin the tiny square in place. (The small squares cover the stitches joining the patches together.)

17 Rolling the bias fold over the edge of the patterned patch, hem the bias edge so that the stitches go through the patterned patch and hold it in place but do not go through to the back of the main patch. Repeat this step three times. When hemming the bias folds, as you reach each corner take two firm stitches to hold the folds together and then continue along the remaining sides (*figure 38*).

18 A pincushion needs only four patches joined in the foregoing manner.

19 Turn the corners of the completed piece to the back as if making an envelope. Join from three corners to the centre with over-sewing.

20 Place small patterned squares as before.

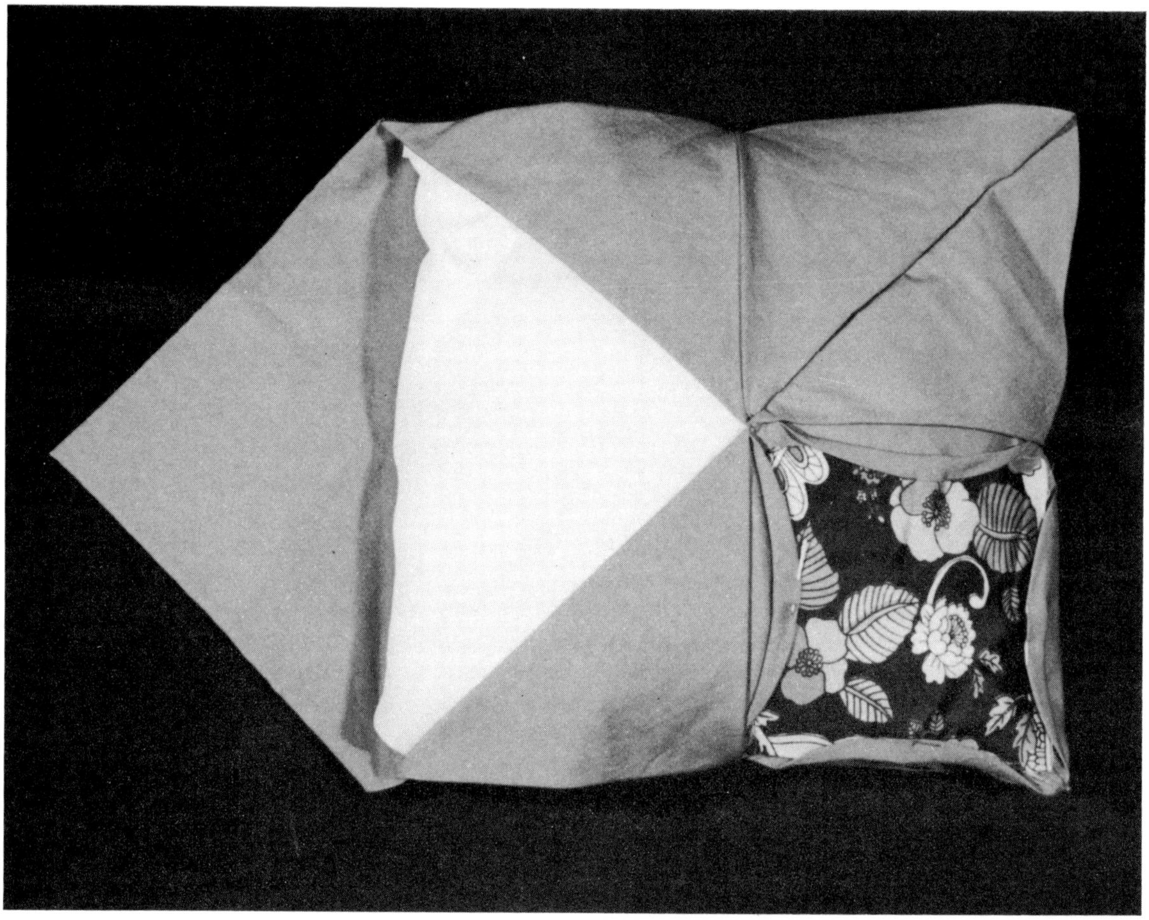

Figure 38 *Cathedral Window patchwork cushion with three points turned to the back. One patterned patch is in place with the bias folds ready for stitching.*

21 Roll the bias edges and stitch as before.

22 Start to sew the remaining opening from the corner to the centre and start stuffing. Continue to close seam until fully stuffed.

23 The last colourful window has to be sewn in place after the pincushion is stuffed. It hides the last seam.

24 Roll the bias edges and stitch.

To make a cushion (*figure 39*)

A cushion approximately 12 in. (30 cm) square needs four pieces of material 18 in. (45 cm) square and a cushion pad is more suitable, as shown in figure 39, than loose stuffing.

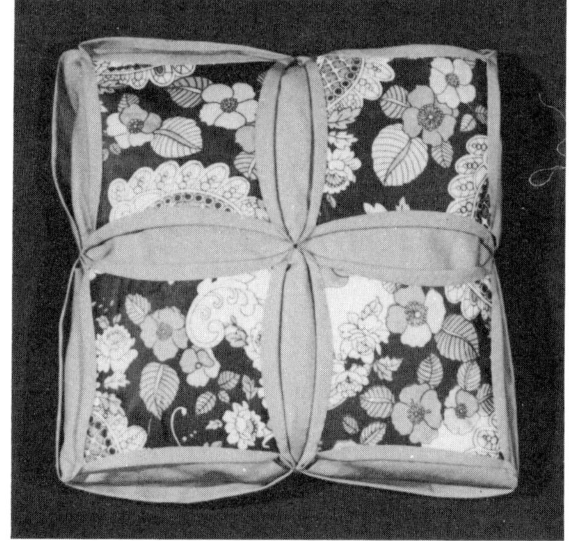

Figure 39 *Completed Cathedral Window patchwork cushion.*

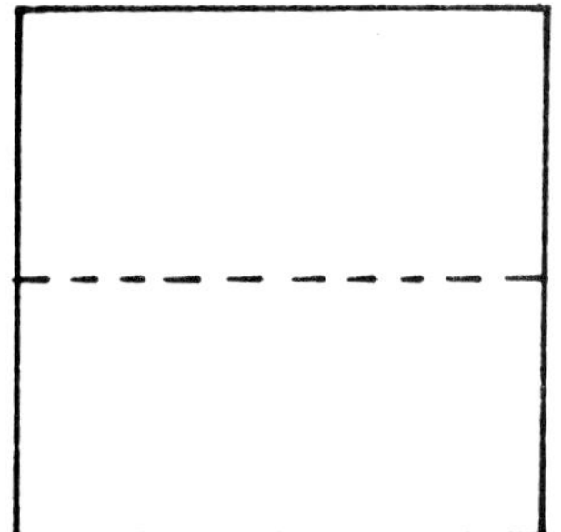

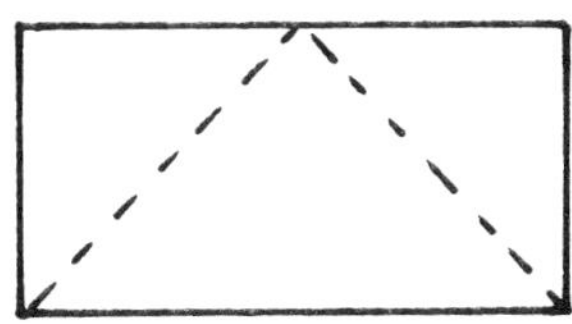

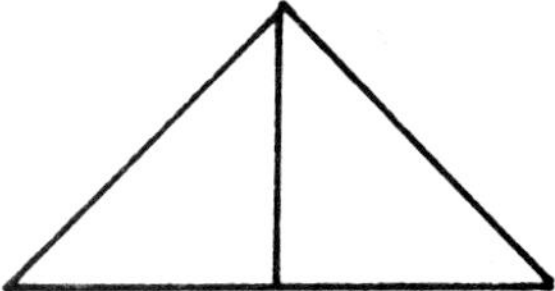

Diagram 28 *How to fold a square of fabric before use in Folded Star patchwork. (Fold on dotted line.)*

Follow steps 1–24 of previous pattern. When stitching the bias folds in patches of this size it is possible to slip your fingers under the folds and it is much easier to do the stitching in this manner.

To make a quilt

The basic technique is the same for a quilt or any other article. You make a large flat piece as required. The size of the original squares will vary to suit your needs – 8–12 in. (20–30 cm) is usually considered adequate.

Folded Star patchwork

Pot holder (*figure 40*)

You may know this way of making a pot holder or a table mat. The measurements given will make a round one 8 in. (20 cm) in diameter.

You will require:

One piece of backing material to make a 9 in. (22·5 cm) circle. Mark the centre point.

Four different fabrics to make the points of the star. Each round of points is a different colour or shade. The points are folded as in diagram 28.

Round 1 Make four points using 3½ in. (8·75 cm) squares of material. Set the four points on the backing material with the points touching at the centre point and the folded edges touching. Stitch the points together and stitch along raw edges of the four folded sections to hold in place. Sew a few stitches near the points, between the folds to hold the points firmly to the backing.

Round 2 Make eight points as before using 5 in. (12·5 cm) squares. Place four of them in the same position as in Round 1, but the points should be ⅝ in. (1·5 cm) from the centre point. Place another four with the points also ⅝ in. (1·5 cm) from the centre point but with the centre line resting on the join between the four sections in the previous row. It is good to have the corners of the sections alternately over and under each other (*figure 40*).

Round 3 Make eight points as before, using 7 in. (17·5 cm) squares. Set exactly as previous row but with points 1¼ in. (3·1 cm) from the centre point.

Round 4 Make eight points as before using 6 in. (15 cm) squares of material and set and stitch as previously. The points should be 1⅞ in. (4·7 cm) from the centre point.

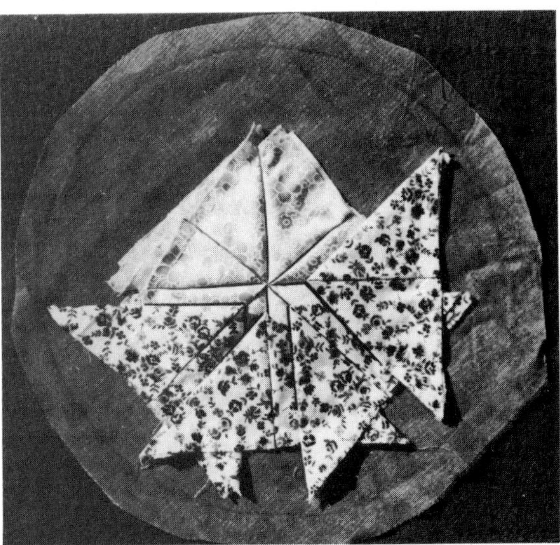

Figure 40 *Detail to show placing of pieces in Folded Star patchwork and Water Lily mat.*

Figure 41 *Folded Star pot-holder.*

Trim the piece of work to a 8 in. (20 cm) circle. Make sure that all outer edges will be held with stitching. Place a piece of material for lining on back of circle. Bind edges with a bias strip. If it is to be used as a pot holder make a loop and attach (*figure 41*).

Water-lily table mat (*figure 42*)

If a piece of work is made in almost the same manner as the foregoing instructions, but leaving the points free, the result as shown in figure 42 makes a stunning table mat.

The edge is finished with a bias strip 4–5 in. (10–12·5 cm) wide and the length is the measurement around the circle (taken $\frac{1}{2}$ in. [1·25 cm] inside the edge. To do this stand your tape measure on edge). The ends of the strip should be joined and then the strip folded in half. Machine stitch $\frac{1}{4}$ in. (6 mm) inside the folded edge. The raw edges of binding and mat

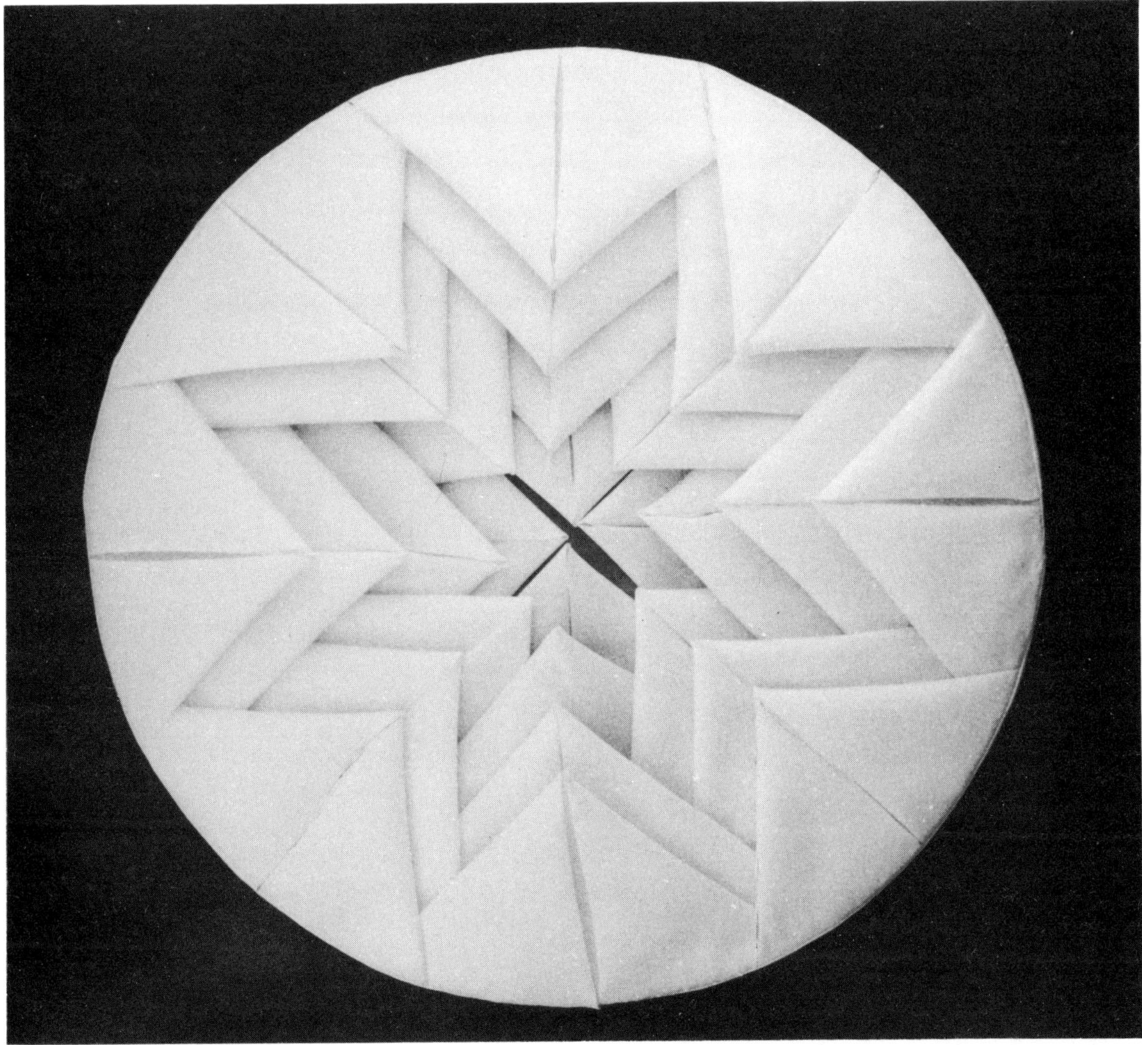

Figure 42 *Water Lily table mat.*

are pinned and stitched $\frac{1}{2}$ in. (1·25 cm) inside the edge.

Thread fine elastic through the folded edge and draw up so that the edge of the sections – the 'petals' – sit on the perimeter of the circle and the binding sits firmly underneath.

A cork mat will sit snugly inside the bias fold.

Imagine a set of these mats with a pale creamy yellow lining slipped under the centre points. It needs to be about 2 in. (5 cm) square. The petals could be cream shading out to pink. They would look like water lilies on a luncheon table. Organdie would be a lovely material to use.

The example in figure 42 is made of synthetic materials which will wash easily and needs no ironing.

6 Strip patchwork

Log Cabin patchwork

One of the foremost exponents of this type of patchwork is Australian Barbara Macey from Melbourne. Hers is a new approach to an old technique (*figure 43*). Since 1973 she has worked exclusively in this technique (*figures 44a and 44b and colour plates 3 and 4*). I am an ardent admirer of her work and it is with pleasure and pride that I publish the following notes by her. There are examples of her work in the Queensland Art Gallery, the Western Australian Gallery and the Victorian State Craft Collection.

New approaches to Log Cabin patchwork

At first sight, the traditional Log Cabin patchwork would seem to be a medium that has little to offer the worker interested in developing new forms. After all, there have been a number of popular variations such as the Courthouse Steps and Pineapple Quilts. Less well-known ideas have been used too, including setting blocks diagonally, using six-sided blocks with the strips of fabric placed around a hexagon instead of a square, and using blocks that are worked from one corner instead of from the centre.

Although these forms have moved away from the original concept of the little log cabin with the red 'fire' at its hearth the traditional name persists.

The main pre-requisites for exploring the possibilities of Log Cabin patchwork are thorough familiarity with traditional block designs, and the use of a technique that is both flexible and accurate enough to be adapted to a block of any rectangular proportions. To help readers to acquire this familiarity and a suitable technique, instructions are given for three basic blocks: Log Cabin, Corner Start and Courthouse Steps (*diagram 29*).

Each block measures 7 in. (17·5 cm) square, and any number of blocks can be assembled to make a cushion, a Tote bag or a quilt of any size. It is important to remember that there is no significance in making a block measuring 7 in. (17·5 cm) square. The Log Cabin block can be of any convenient size. General instructions for assembling blocks are also given. Since accuracy and flexibility are primary considerations, directions are given for ruling lines on the calico backing as a guide to strip placement. You will need:

a ruler

a very sharp 2B pencil and a knife for frequent sharpening

a newspaper

a $\frac{3}{4}$ in. (2 cm) wide strip of cardboard with a straight edge

a piece of dressmakers' carbon paper, dark blue or red

and for each block: two strips of fabric, each $2\frac{3}{4}$ in. (7 cm) long by the full width of fabric, one light coloured, one dark.

Figure 43 *'Stellar', made by Barbara Macey © 1973.*

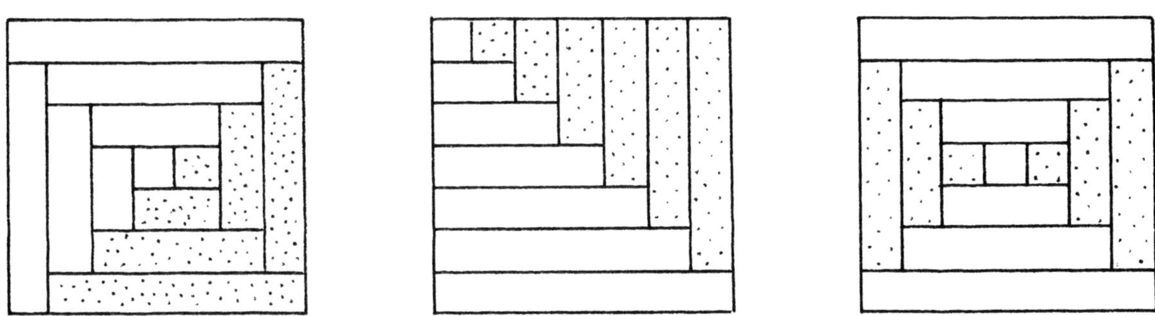

Diagram 29 *Three traditional blocks.* From left to right: *Log Cabin; Corner Start; Courthouse Steps.*

Selection and preparation of fabrics

It should be noted that the character of Log Cabin patchwork is permanently changed when the piece is laundered, due to the strips becoming slightly puffed or puckered, an effect that many people find pleasing. It has been suggested that this may be caused by changes in the sewing thread. A different kind of puckering that is potentially damaging occurs when an article made of fabric that was not pre-shrunk is laundered. Shrinkage at this stage places fabric under tension, which could eventually weaken and tear it. To avoid this problem, all fabrics including calico, lining, binding and cords must be washed before use; remember if the dye runs, don't use that fabric.

Figure 44a *'Houndstooth', made by Barbara Macey © 1980.*

Figure 44b *Detail of* 44a. *Note the intricate placing of the pieces in what is still basically Log Cabin patchwork. We counted 45 different black and white prints in the work.*

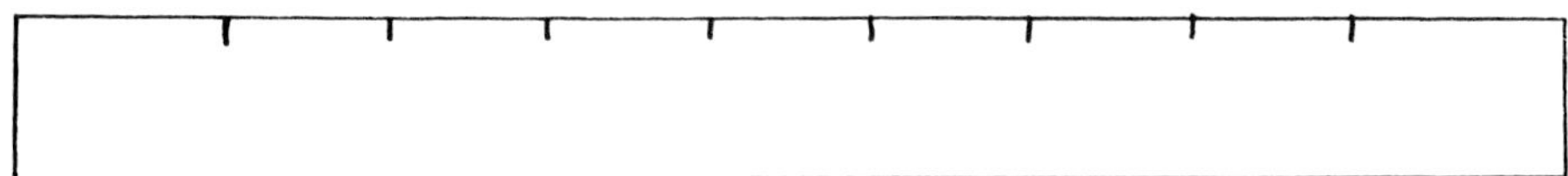

Diagram 30 *A gauge is easily made by appropriately marking a strip of cardboard with positions of the marks to be ruled on the calico.*

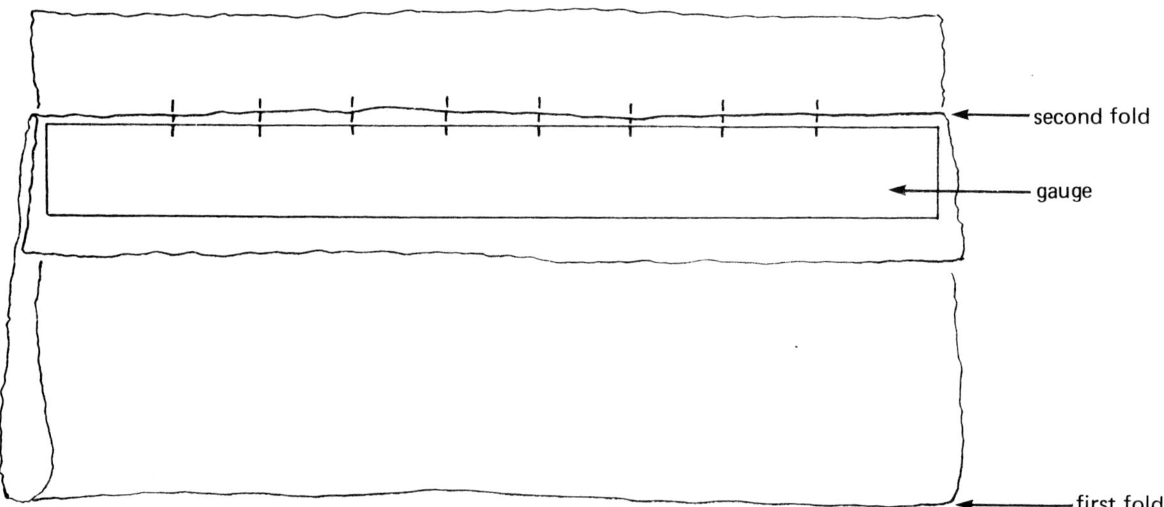

Diagram 31 *The gauge correctly placed on the folded calico square, which has been marked with the positions for the grid lines.*

Preparing the calico backing

Preparation is the same for all three blocks. To allow for seams when setting finished blocks together, the calico backing for the strips must be larger than the block being made. The blocks in this section have a finished size of 7 in. (17·5 cm) each way, therefore the calico backing must be at least 8½ in. (21·25 cm) square, for a seam allowance of ¾ in. (2 cm). Cut and press the calico. A grid of pencilled lines can be marked on the calico using a ruler, but there is less chance of error if a cardboard gauge is used (*diagram 30*).

Make sure that there are only eight marks, with seven spaces between them; each space will measure 1 in. (2·5 cm). The first and last marks are for the seamlines, to be used as a guide when sewing blocks together. The rest indicate places where fabric strips will be sewn. Place a piece of newspaper on the table to make a non-slip surface. The calico is folded so that the grid lines can be marked on opposite edges in the one operation (*diagram 31*). Fold the calico crosswise so that the opposite edges are even, and facing away from you. Now fold about 1 in. (2·5 cm) of the edge of the upper layer towards you and make a crease. Place the gauge so that it is on top of this second fold, but leaving the creased edge free.

The first mark should be ¾ in. (2 cm) inside the edge of the calico. Holding the gauge firmly, transfer all eight marks to the creased edge of the top layer of calico, and the layer beneath it (*diagram 31*).

Unfold the calico, and connect each mark with the one opposite using a ruler, held firmly. Take all lines to the edge of the calico, as in diagram 32a. A very light touch with the pencil is imperative to avoid stretching the calico. Use a very sharp pencil at all times. Repeat this procedure, using the gauge to make two more sets of marks as before along the previously

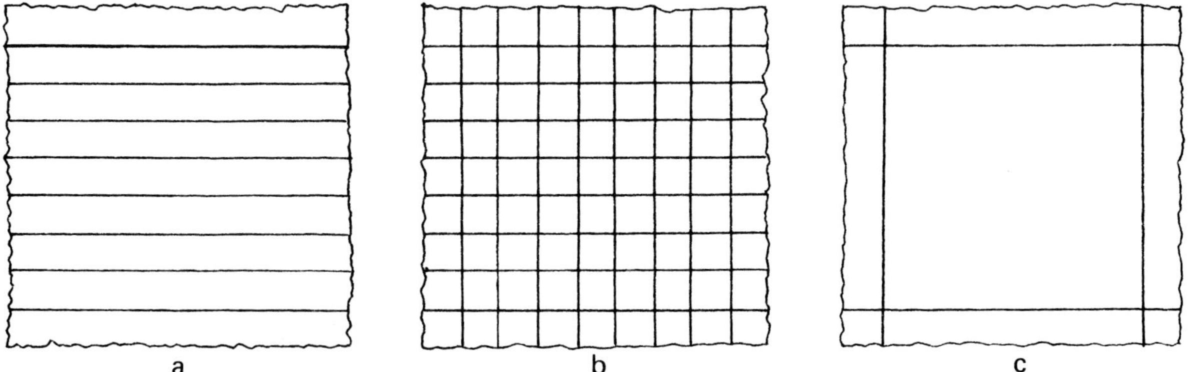

Diagram 32 *The calico square with:* a *the first set of lines ruled;* b *the grid completed;* c *the back of the square with seam lines marked by placing dressmakers' carbon paper under the calico before ruling the last line of each side of the grid.*

drawn seam lines, so that there is another set of marks at right angles to the first (*diagram 32b*). The lines drawn so far are all on the right side of the calico, where the strips will be sewn, therefore they will be of no use for setting the finished blocks together. Lines on the wrong side are needed for this, and they are easily transferred with dressmaker's carbon paper. Take the paper, and place it, carbon side up, on the working surface, and place the calico over it, right side up. Rule once more over the seam-lines only (*diagram 32c*).

Preparing the strips

First calculate how wide the pieces of fabric must be. To do this, double the finished width of the strip and add $\frac{3}{4}$ in. (2 cm) for seam allowance. For example, if the finished width of a strip is to be 1 in. (2·5 cm), then you need a piece of fabric $2\frac{3}{4}$ in. (7 cm) wide. It is best to tear off a piece of fabric wide enough to make two strips. In this case, it will be $5\frac{1}{2}$ in. (14 cm). With this fabric, fold in half lengthwise, then press. Cut along the crease. Again, fold each piece in half lengthwise and press. The strips are now ready to use.

For very heavy fabrics use single width. To calculate this add $\frac{3}{4}$ in. (2 cm) to finished width of the strip. For example if the finished width is to be 1 in. (2·5 cm) then it must be $1\frac{3}{4}$ in. (4·5 cm) wide.

Cutting and placing the strips

Now you are ready to cut and place the strips according to your chosen design.

Before sewing, place all strips in correct order on the backing to see the effect. If it is unsatisfactory, changes are easy to make at this stage.

Remove selvedges before cutting the prepared strip.

The order of strip placement in these three blocks is indicated by the numbers (*diagram 33* and *figure 45*).

The first strip, no matter where it is placed, is prepared a little differently from the rest, as it needs an additional seam allowance. Cut a $3\frac{1}{2}$ in. (9 cm) length from the appropriate strip, press open, and trim 1 in. (2·5 cm) from one long edge. Fold it at right angles to previous fold, to form a $1\frac{3}{4}$ in. (4·5 cm) square. Press. Place this strip over the appropriate square of the grid, centres matched (*diagram 34a*).

The second strip is the same length as the first, in this case $1\frac{3}{4}$ in. (4·5 cm). Place it over the seam allowance of the first strip, the fold aligned with the correct grid line on the calico (*diagram 34b*).

For Courthouse Steps arrangement, the third strip is the same length as the second. For the Log Cabin and Corner Start blocks the third strip is the same length as the first and second strips as they are placed (overlapped) on the calico. Another way of saying this is that each strip is the length of the section of grid it is to cover, plus $\frac{3}{4}$ in. (2 cm) seam allowance. Continue to cut and place strips in this manner until all 13 are in place on the calico (*diagrams 34b,*

Figure 45 *Basic Log Cabin sampler, made by Barbara Macey.*

34c, *34d*, *34e* and *34f*). The folded edge of each strip must always face the centre.

For large projects, it is wise to cut strips for a number of blocks to be sure that the effect is to your satisfaction. Remember that the predominant shapes seen in a large area are often unexpected, and that slight changes in the light-dark distribution can make a great difference to the final result. The calico squares with their unsewn strips can easily be stored by stacking on a piece of cardboard, and then slipping them carefully into a plastic bag.

Hand sewing the strips to the calico

When you are ready to start sewing, take a prepared block, and remove the strips from the calico, starting with the longest one and working back to the smallest, which should now be on top of the pile. For hand sewing, take a size 8 needle, and fine thread to match the strip you are sewing. Place the first strip over the appropriate square of the grid, centre matched, and tack into position. By tacking the edges of the

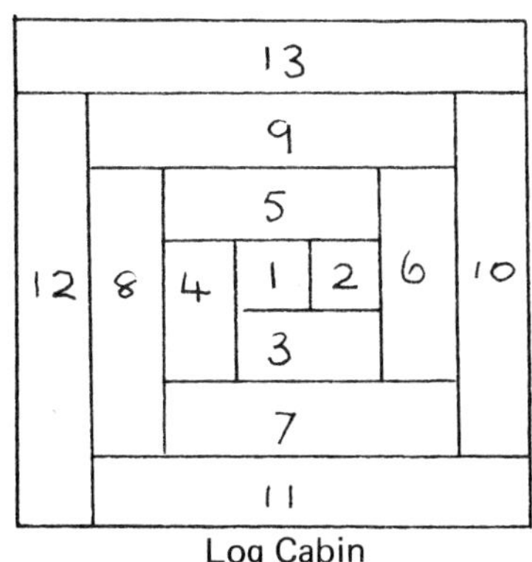

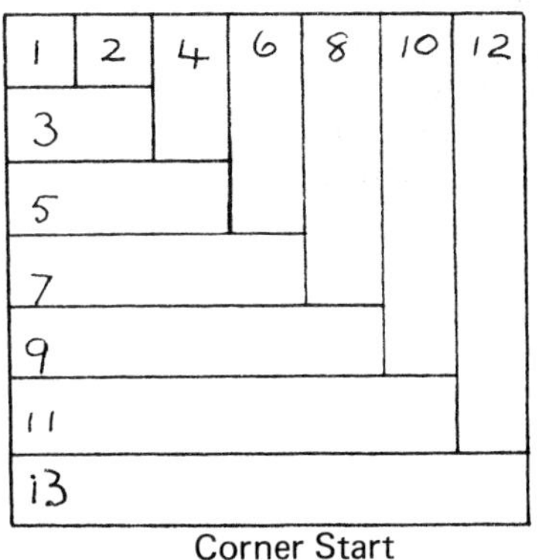

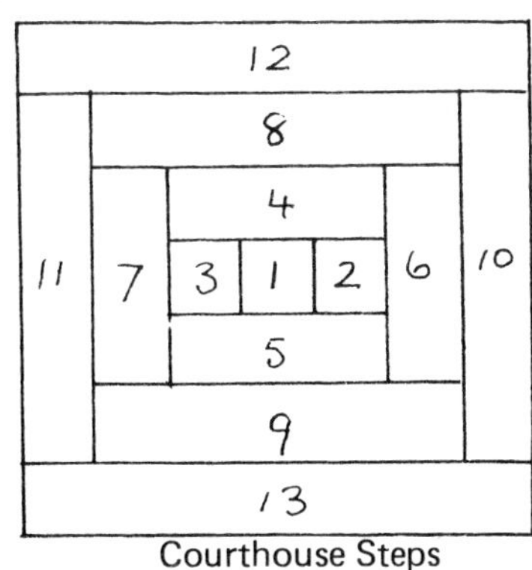

Diagram 33 *Strip placement is indicated by the numbers on the Log Cabin, Corner Start and Courthouse Steps blocks.*

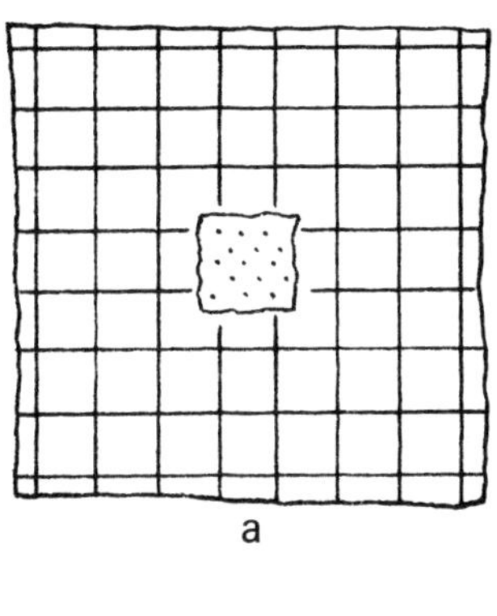

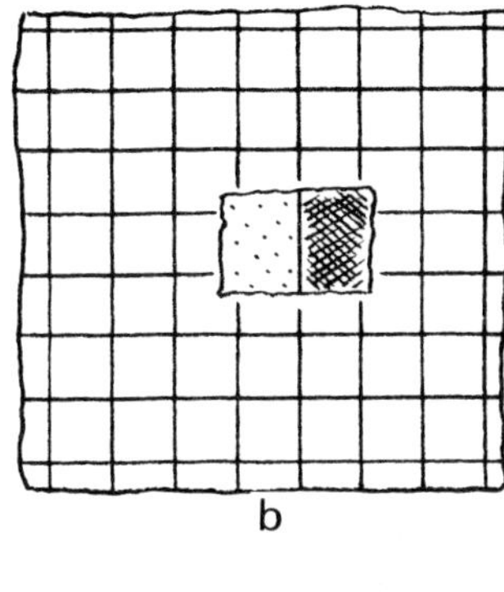

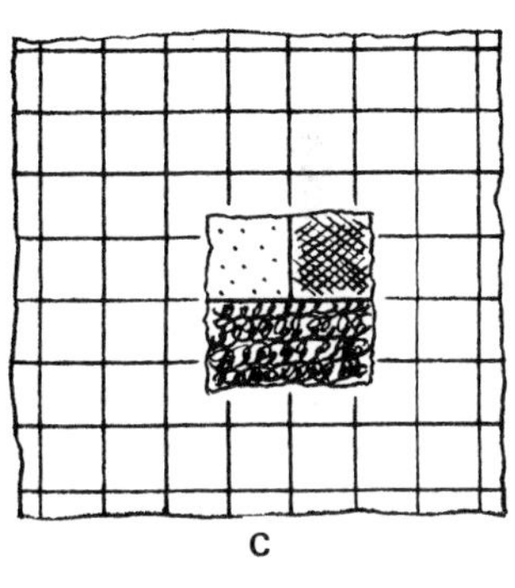

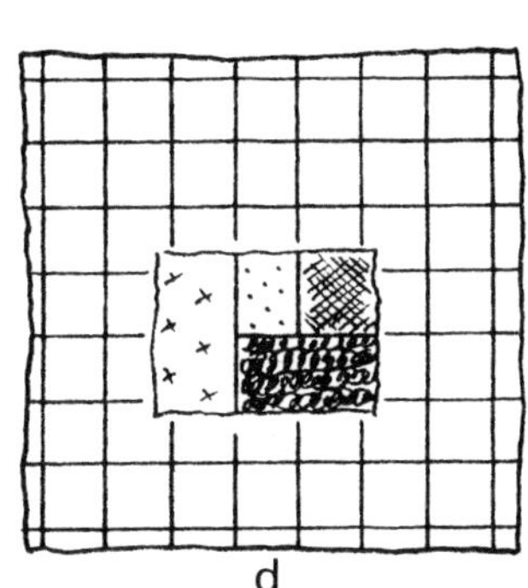

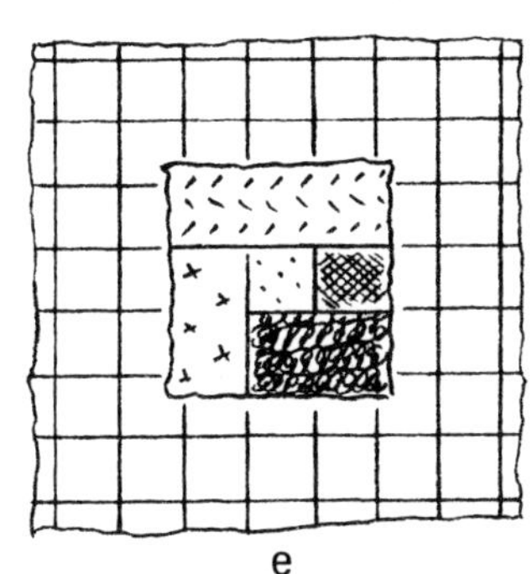

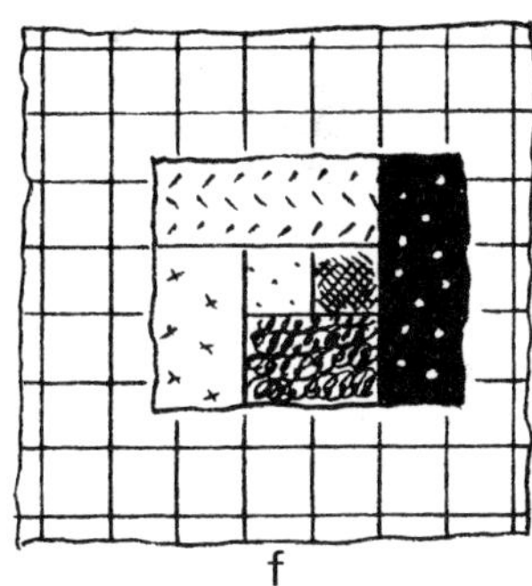

Diagram 34 *These drawings show how the fabric strips are placed in sequence, each covering the raw edges of the one before.*

first strip in the same sequence as the following strips will be placed, the needle is brought to the correct position for sewing the second strip in position (*diagram 35a*). Place the second strip where it will be sewn, open, and carefully align the crease with the grid, pin in place and sew with a small running stitch (*diagram 35b*). Fold the strip back into place.

So far, these instructions apply to all three blocks, but the arrangement of strips in the 'Corner Start' and 'Courthouse Steps' blocks, calls for the stitching to be finished off after every second strip and every strip respectively. For 'Log Cabin' and 'Corner Start', tack along the end of the strip just sewn, from the folded to the raw edge, so that the needle is in the correct position to sew the third strip in position (*diagram 35c*). Open the third strip, align, pin in place, and stitch. Continue in this manner until all thirteen strips have been sewn to the calico (*diagram 35d*). Press carefully.

Using the sewing machine

Strips are sewn to the calico in exactly the same manner as described for hand sewing, but the thread is not changed to match each fabric. Instead match thread to the colour of the lightest fabric, as dark thread often shows through light-coloured fabrics.

Use a medium needle, and set stitch length regulator so that the machine is sewing about eight stitches per inch (about four stitches per centimetre). To avoid damage to fabric if unpicking becomes necessary, always work from the wrong side of the calico. Unpicked strips can be used again if the needle holes are removed by washing, but some fabrics must be discarded. When machining, the work needs frequent pressing to keep the strips flat.

Joining the blocks by hand

Joining two blocks together requires accurate pinning. Place the blocks right sides together. Where the seam lines intersect on the wrong sides of the calico, place a pin perpendicular to the fabric, through all layers, so that it emerges at the corresponding intersections on the second block. Place another pin in the same way through the intersection lines at the other end of the seamline. These pins are only to align the seam correctly for conventional pinning (*diagram 36a*).

Where these first two pins are located, pin at right angles to the direction of the seam to be sewn. Remove the two aligning pins. If there are any places where the ends of the strips meet on adjacent blocks, use this method of aligning, then pinning the fabric to match them correctly. Pin the rest of the seamline, but place the pins along (not across) the seamline. Make certain that they pass through the seamlines on both front and back pieces of calico (*diagram 36b*). Use a back stitch for this seam stabbing the needle in and out in two separate movements so

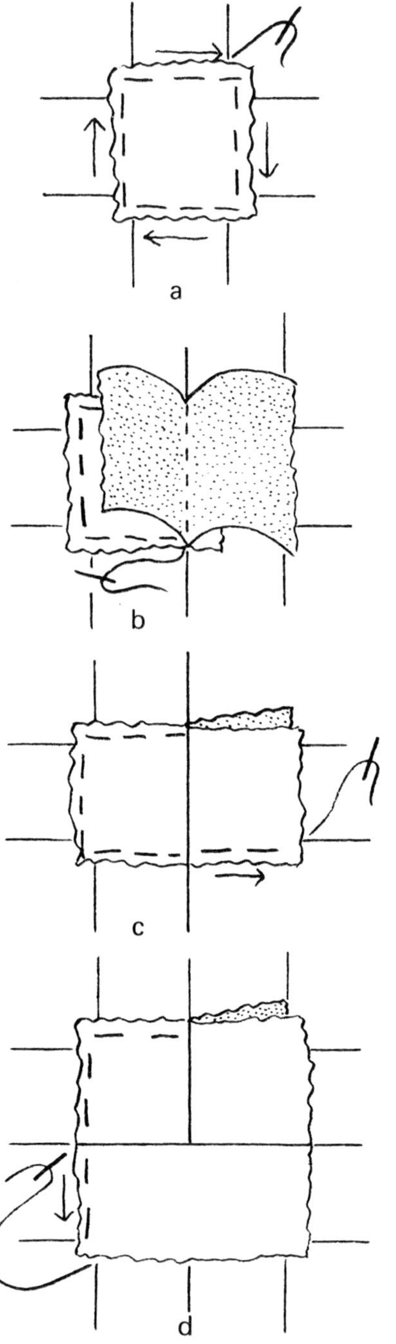

Diagram 35a *The first step of the fabric is placed on the appropriate square of the grid and then tacked in place;* b *the second strip is sewn in place with small running stitches;* c *the strip is folded away from the first one and held in place with a few tacking stitches across the end;* d *the third strip is added in the same way.*

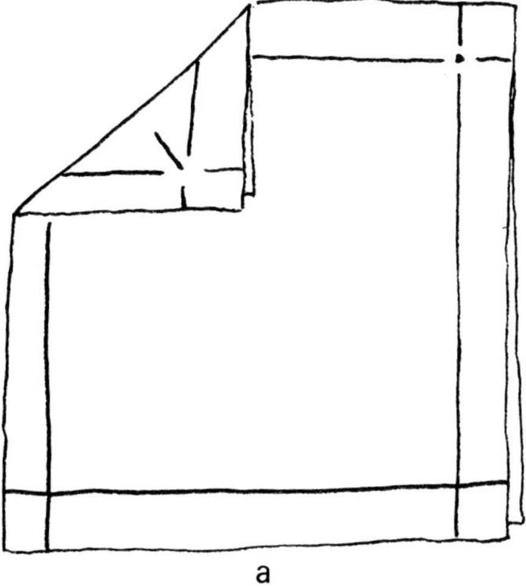

a

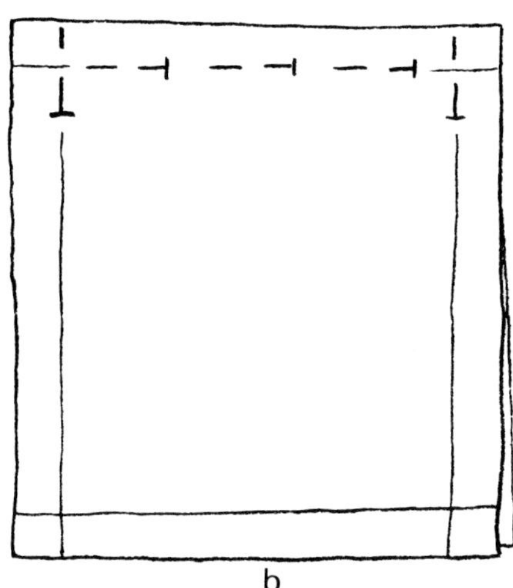

b

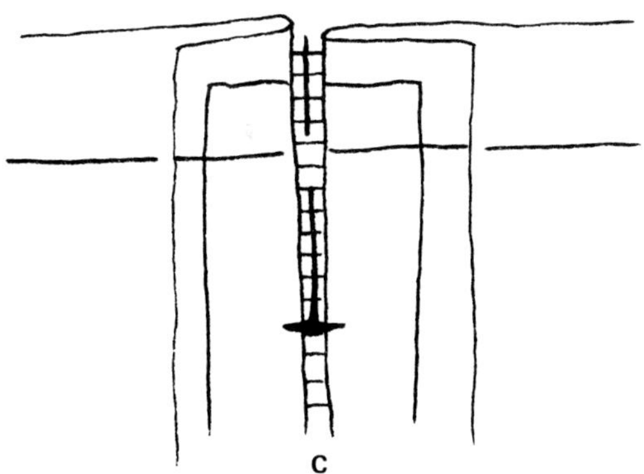

c

that the fabric layers are not disturbed. Pay attention to the back of the work as you do this, or the stitches will wander from the seamline.

Continue joining the blocks in rows. To join two rows together, first make any necessary adjustments to those seamlines that appear crooked, and continue all seamlines across the seams you have pressed open. Place the rows of blocks, right sides together, with cross seams corresponding. At each pair of cross seams place a pin perpendicular to the fabric passing it through the seam channel between the stitches without piercing the fabric. Secure by pinning across the seam between the stitches only (*diagram 36c*). Remove the first pin. Place pins along the rest of the seam to secure it accurately in place. Sew in the same way as for joining two blocks together, being very careful to keep cross seams in alignment.

Joining the blocks by machine

The work is pinned exactly as for hand sewing. Sew back a few stitches at both ends of all seams for security. Work carefully to avoid bunching and inaccurate stitching, removing pins as you go. Never allow bunches and pleats to remain in the calico backing, as they will show on the front of the work. Bunching can be controlled easily by applying tension to the work as it passes under the presser foot. Take great care to allow the fabric to feed naturally through the machine, as forcing it can damage the needle, or the machine mechanism. You may prefer simply to raise the work before it passes under the presser foot. These two manoeuvres usually work well, but sometimes the fabric bunches badly and it is necessary to stop the machine frequently to ease back the top layer of fabric.

To sew two rows of blocks together, pin as for hand sewing. Stitch along the seamline to within $\frac{1}{4}$ in. (6 mm) of the first cross seam. Stop, raise the needle and the presser foot. Keeping

Diagram 36a *When seaming blocks together seams are aligned by placing pins through the seam intersections at right angles to the fabric;* b *pins are placed across the seam in the same position and the aligning pins are removed. More pins are placed along the rest of the seam;* c *at seam intersections, pins pass between stitches, not through the fabric.*

the pin that secures the cross seams in place, move the work back until the needle is directly over the cross seams. Lower the needle between the stitches securing these seams, so that it does not pass through the fabric. Lower the presser foot and sew back a few stitches, a little beyond where you stopped machining. Sew forward over the pin. Repeat this procedure at each cross seam. Check the finished seam for accuracy. If it is satisfactory, press the seam open, spraying with a little water. Press the right side too. If the seam is not properly matched, unpick this section and correct the fault.

Large articles

The sort of work we have been discussing so far, can be sewn by machine quite easily, using either a cabinet model or a portable model.

Large articles should be assembled in several equal sections of a size that can be handled under your usual sewing conditions. To complete the assembly, lining and binding of the quilt, it is a great advantage to set up a temporary work area using your small machine table, a large table and an ironing board, so that the weight of the quilt can be supported at all times. This avoids damage to the machine and inaccurate and uneven stitching. Place the large table away from all walls, with the sewing table half way along the long side and at right angles to it. The ironing board goes at the opposite side, its long side against the large table. The bulk of the quilt remains on the table at all times, until it is finished. As there are already several thicknesses of fabric, this type of patchwork does not need batting. Neither does it need to be quilted because the technique of applying strips to a calico base constitutes quilting. It is sufficient to provide a lining, secured at each seam intersection with a few stitches on top of each other (known as tacking). This lining should be a little larger than the quilt to prevent the edges from rolling under.

Binding is a good way to finish. So that the seam line markings can be used, it should be sewn to the right side of the quilt before the lining is in place and hand-sewn to the back, through both lining and calico, after the lining is tacked to the patchwork.

It is useful to know how much fabric to buy for a large article. The following table is a rough guide that can be used as a basis for calculations. It is for strips of 1 in. (2·5 cm) finished width. If narrower strips are used more fabric will be needed. The amount of material required is calculated for 36 in. (90 cm) wide fabric.

Number of squares	*Size of squares*	*Material required*
4	7 in. (17·5 cm)	24 in. (60 cm)
4	8 in. (20 cm)	32 in. (80 cm)
4	9 in. (22·5 cm)	36 in. (90 cm)
4	10 in. (25 cm)	44 in. (1·10 m)
4	11 in. (27·5 cm)	52 in. (1·30 m)
4	12 in. (30 cm)	63 in. (1·60 m)

These amounts should be equally divided between the two groupings.

At this rate, you would need approximately 5 yds (4·5 m) of fabric 36 in. (90 cm) wide to cover a square metre of patchwork in 1 in. (2·5 cm) strips, or 24 in. (60 cm) of fabric (or equivalent in scraps) to cover a 14 in. (35 cm) square cushion on one side only.

When buying fabric for large articles such as quilts it is best to buy an extra metre of the predominant fabrics to allow for mistakes and shrinkage. If most strips in all blocks are very narrow, you will need to make a prototype block to see how much fabric is needed to cover it. The amount of backing fabric needed must be calculated, too. One metre of 36 in. (90 cm) wide calico yields:

Number of backing pieces	*Size of squares*
16	7 in. (17·5 cm)
12	8 in. (20 cm)
9	9 in. (22·5 cm)
9	10 in. (25 cm)
6	11 in. (27·5 cm)
4	12 in. (30 cm)

Do not forget to buy fabric for binding and lining as the same fabric may not be available later. For some designs it is best to make a prototype and calculate quantities.

Beyond traditional Log Cabin patchwork

So far we have discussed three Log Cabin patchwork blocks. Two of them, 'Log Cabin' and 'Courthouse Steps' are often seen in quilts worked in the traditional manner; the third, 'Corner Start', is rarely encountered. On examining a number of traditional quilts, it is apparent that, although the maker was probably unaware of it, the design has been dictated by a set of widely accepted conventions. This has a limiting effect. Let us look at these conventions and some ways of modifying them.

Diagram 37 *Two rectangular grids (* c *and* f*) with designs that can be worked from them (* a, b, d *and* e*). There are many other possibilities.*

Convention 1: All blocks must be square. This is not so. Square blocks can be stretched horizontally or vertically into a rectangle of any proportions. This means that either the width or the placement of strips must be changed (*diagram 37*).

The four blocks shown in diagram 37 are traditional blocks that have been 'stretched' vertically. In diagram 37a and diagram 37b the vertical strips have been elongated to fit the rectangle. All strips remain 1 in. (2·5 cm) wide. On the other hand, in diagram 37d and diagram 37e the horizontal strips are widened to fill the space. These differences are reflected in the two grids (*diagrams 37c and 37f*).

Blocks can also be trimmed to suit irregular shapes (e.g. seat covers or bags). In this case, you can simply make a piece of rectangular patchwork large enough to cut the required

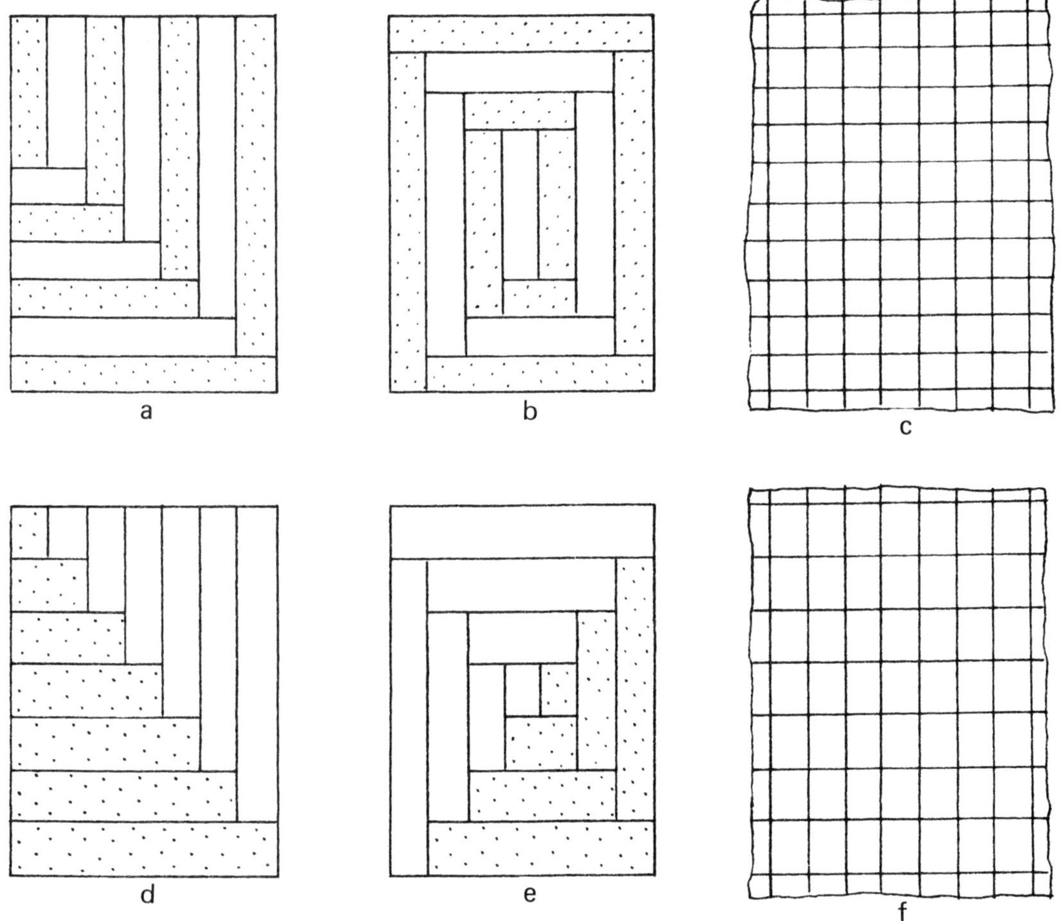

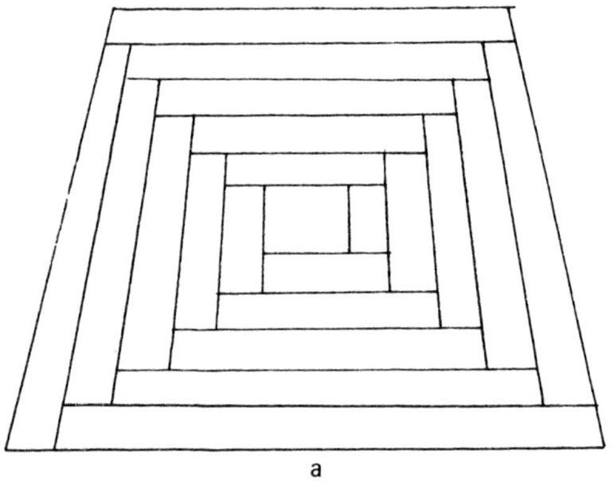

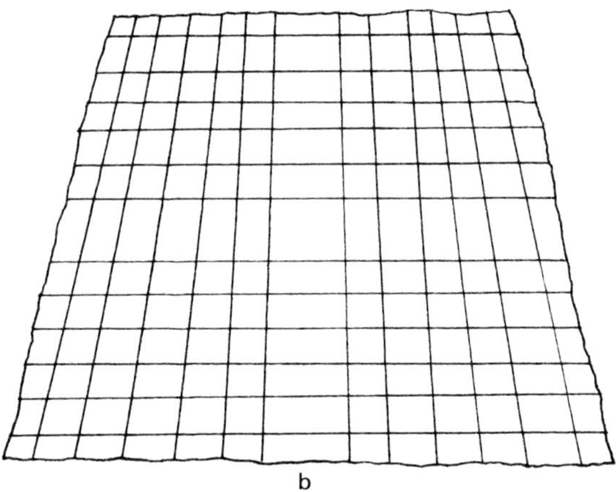

Diagram 38a *An irregular block with its grid (*b*).*

pattern from, or you can fit the strips to the required shape (*diagram 38*).

Diagram 38a shows a design for a shaped seat cover. The appropriate grid is shown in diagram 38b. This sort of shaping can also be used for garments.

Arrows indicate seams. Diagrams 39a and 39c are designs suitable for covers for shaped chair seats. All shaped blocks are first drawn up as rectangular grids and trimmed to shape before the strips are placed. Remember to transfer the new seamline to the wrong side of the calico with dressmakers' carbon paper. Diagram 39b is suitable for a bag.

Convention 2: All blocks must be of equal size. This is incorrect. Squares and rectangles of various sizes can be used in the one article. Again this may require adaptation of strip measurements or numbers (*diagram 40*).

Convention 3: Blocks must be set together in such a way that their seamlines form a network of squares. Not true. Many alternatives to this can be seen in the arrangement of bricks and stones (*diagram 41*).

Convention 4: All strips must be the same width. This is a misconception. Strips of many widths can be used in the one block or article. This concept makes it possible to create a great range of designs. An important implication of using multiple strip widths is that the ends of the strips within a block can be placed along a curved shape. In diagram 42a the ends of the strips fall along a straight line. If you wish the line to be curved, as in diagram 42b, draw one set of lines on the calico (*diagram 42c*) and a second set at right angles, where they intersect with the curve (*diagram 42d*). Sometimes it is necessary to manipulate these sets of lines so that the progression of strip widths is pleasing. Sudden large differences of size can be disturbing. When the grid is complete (*diagram 42d*), sew strips in the order shown in diagram 42e.

A curve worked from a centre start is shown in diagram 42f.

Convention 5: The strips must be arranged in the same order around a central square. Another false notion. A block can be worked from any point within the seamlines, and strips can be placed in any sequence. Here are a few examples. The starting point of all blocks in diagram 43 is indicated by a dot.

Convention 6: All blocks in a piece of work must have identical light and dark areas. Quite wrong. It is not necessary to keep to the triangular light and dark areas traditionally associated with Log Cabin patchwork. Even if the blocks in a quilt are worked in the conventional fashion, a change in the balance of light-dark tones, or the use of intermediate tones can produce an arresting and original piece of work. Below are a few examples of blocks with unconventional distribution of light-dark tones (*diagram 44*).

The grid

For freedom of strip arrangement the grid already described is unsurpassed. Using it means that it is feasible to work the block from any point within the seamlines. It is also poss-

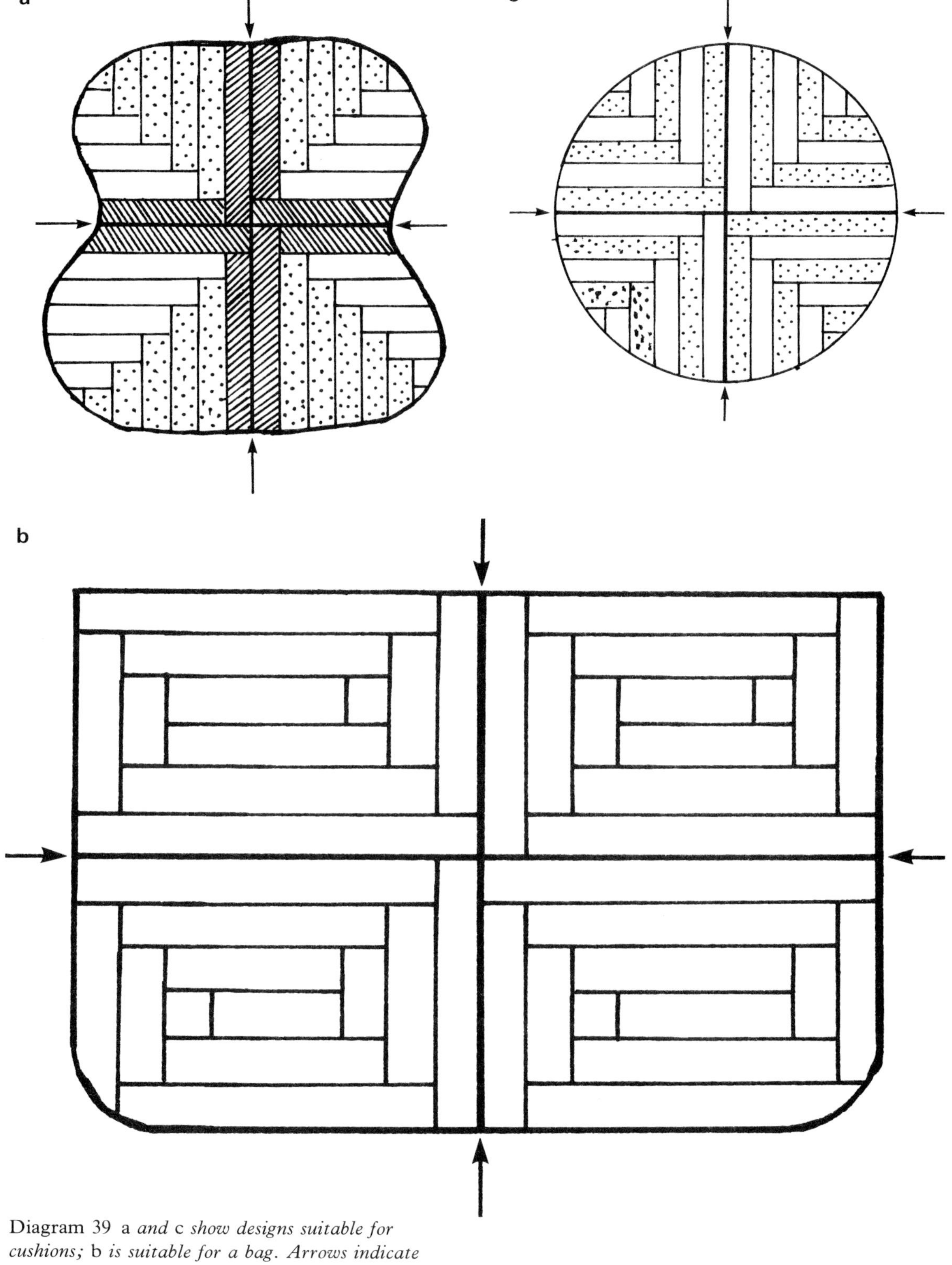

Diagram 39 a *and* c *show designs suitable for cushions;* b *is suitable for a bag. Arrows indicate seam lines.*

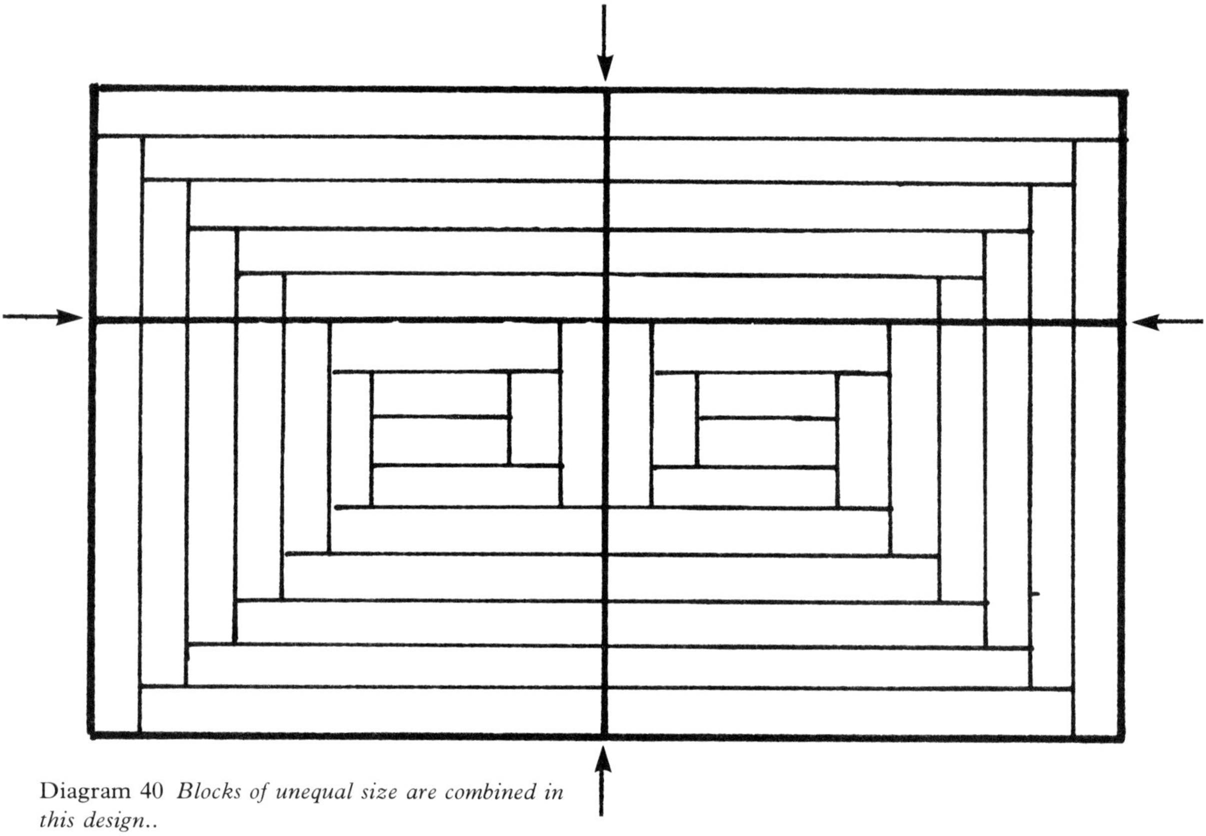

Diagram 40 *Blocks of unequal size are combined in this design..*

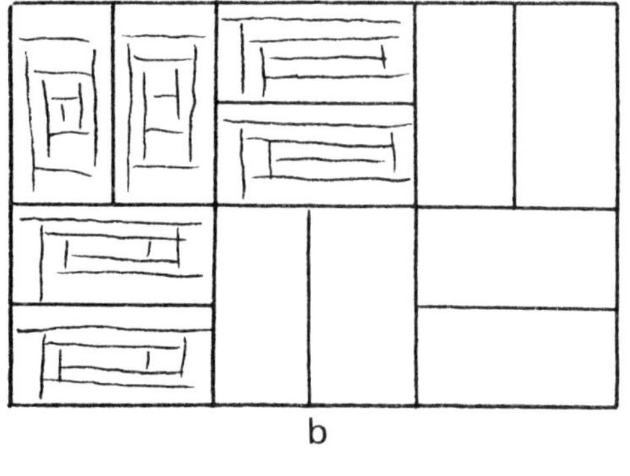

Diagram 41 *Alternate ways of setting blocks together.*

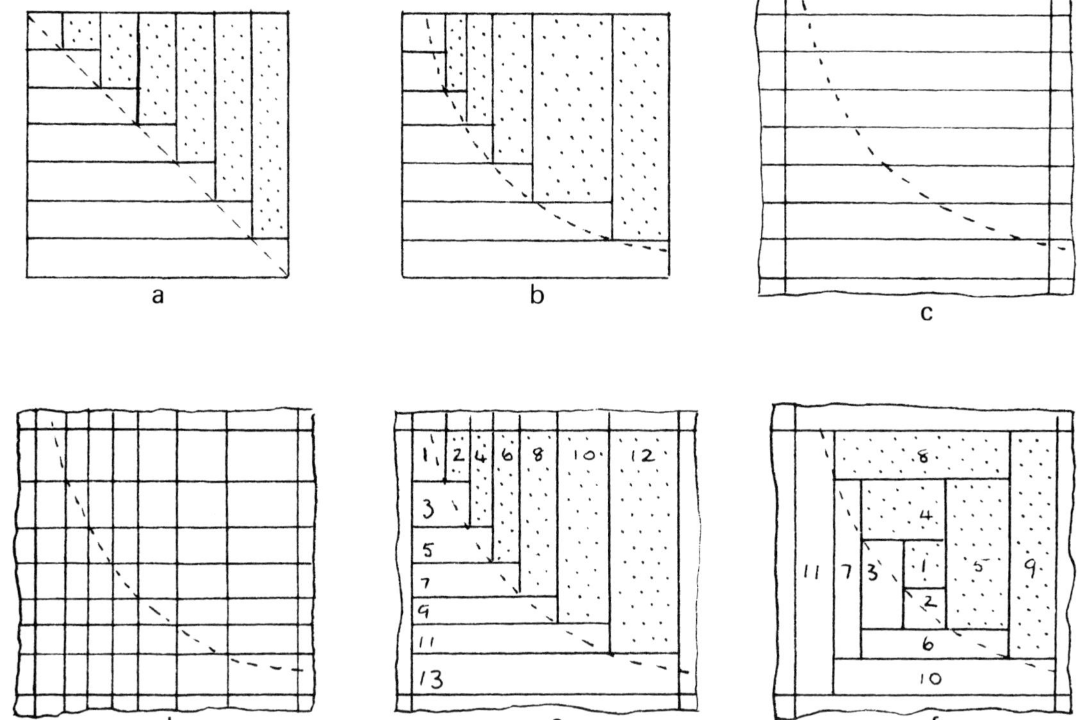

Diagram 42 a *A straight line connects the outer corners of strips of equal width diagonally;* b *when the vertical strips are altered in width, their corners fall along a curve;* c *and* d *the first and second stages of drawing a grid for this block. The horizontal lines are drawn, then the vertical lines are placed where the horizontal lines intersect the curve;* e *both vertical and horizontal lines are irregularly placed in this block;* f *curved shapes can also be worked from the centre of the block.*

ible to use strips of varying widths, as in diagram 42, with no more complex calculations than that for the traditional blocks. This is because it is possible to make a gauge from a full-size drawing of the block design. Hold a strip of cardboard across the block and transfer to it all marks needed for correct placement of strips and seamlines. The gauge can then be used to transfer these marks to the calico as described earlier. Another advantage is that systematic errors in sewing strips in place are kept within the block seamlines. Without this control, the quilt can become appreciably larger or smaller than originally intended. Because the strips are attached to calico, they are under no strain. This means that for non-functional patchwork it is possible to use fabrics that would otherwise be regarded as unsuitable, for example, seersucker, delicate sheers (used double for opacity), mixed weights. No further quilting is necessary as there are already several layers of fabric firmly fixed together. Using the grid also means that it is possible to attempt designs that could not easily be tackled with other techniques. An example of this is seen in diagram 40, where the ends of the strips on adjacent blocks must meet accurately at the seamlines. Even so, this type of design is best avoided by beginners. The shaped seat covers in diagrams 38 and 39 are also easier to make using the grid. It does have one disadvantage; the calico could make the quilt too heavy. In this case, use lawn or an even lighter fabric as a base for the strips. As long as it is crisp it should be satisfactory. Use spray starch before drawing the grid if necessary.

Positive and negative

In some Log Cabin patchwork designs, all blocks are identical with respect to light-dark distribution, but in others, both positive and

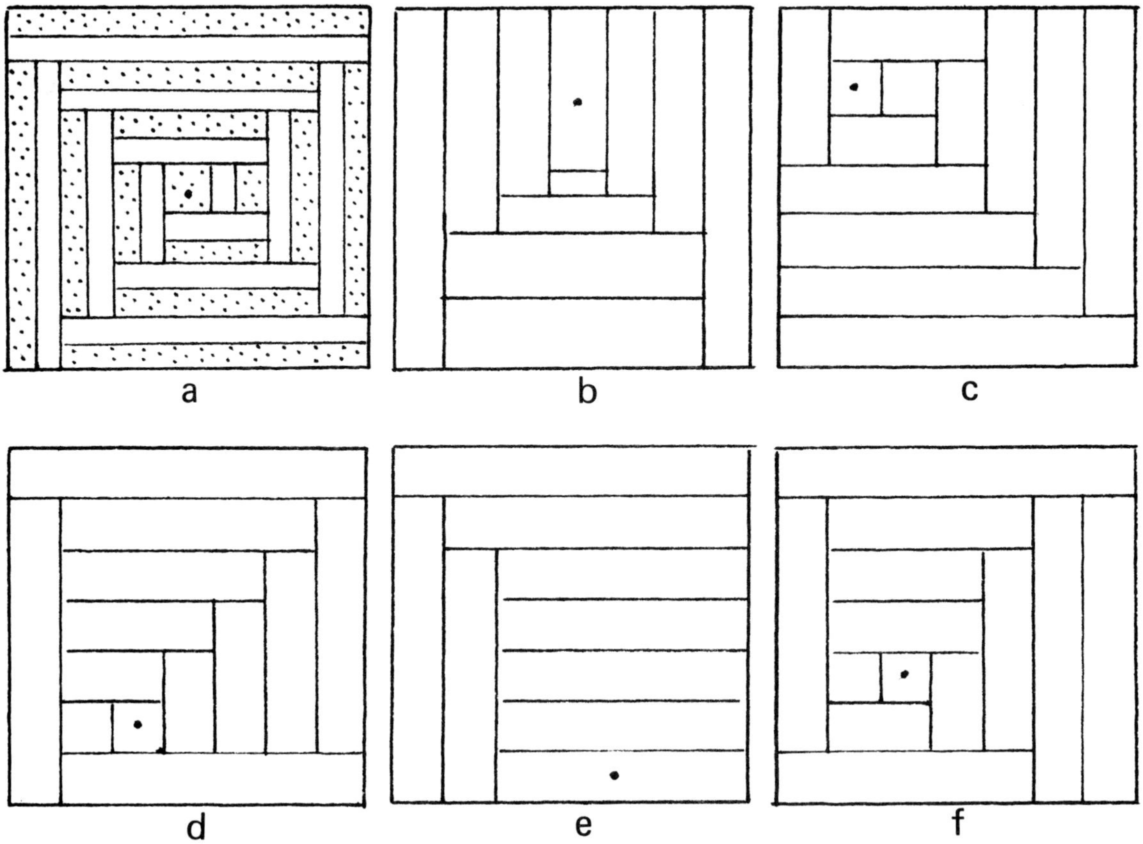

a b c

d e f

Diagram 43a, b, c, d, e *and* f *Designs can be worked from any point within the block. The dot in each block indicates the starting point.*

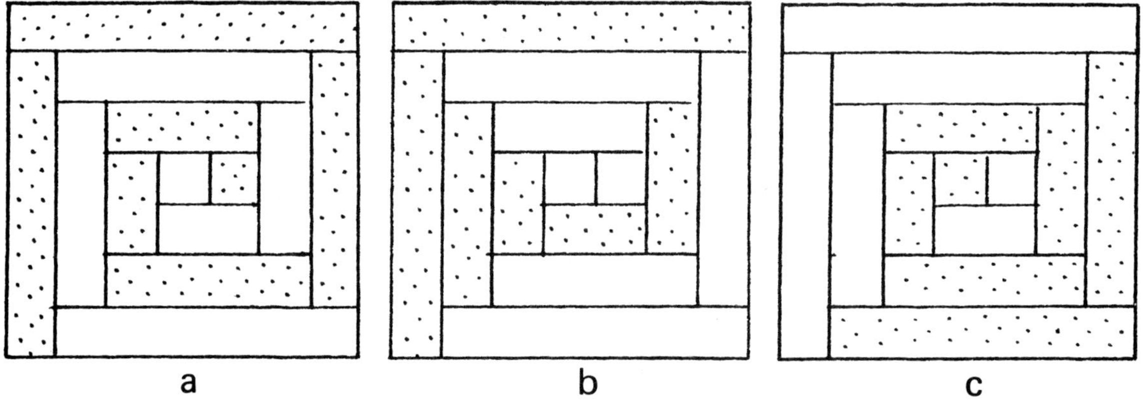

Diagram 44a, b *and* c *Light and dark strips can be arranged in any way desired.*

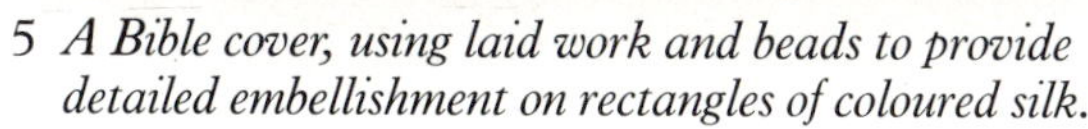

5 *A Bible cover, using laid work and beads to provide detailed embellishment on rectangles of coloured silk.*

6 *Seminole patchwork on an American Indian bag. The strip on the small bag is surprisingly complicated.*

7 *The coals of fire in the embroidered panel 'Firebird' are silk patchwork. Although not all of the same size, they are all derived from hexagons (with the exception of one church window) and with careful placing an irregular pattern of colour is built up.*

8 *The hood of one of the Winchester copes, based on Log Cabin patchwork.*

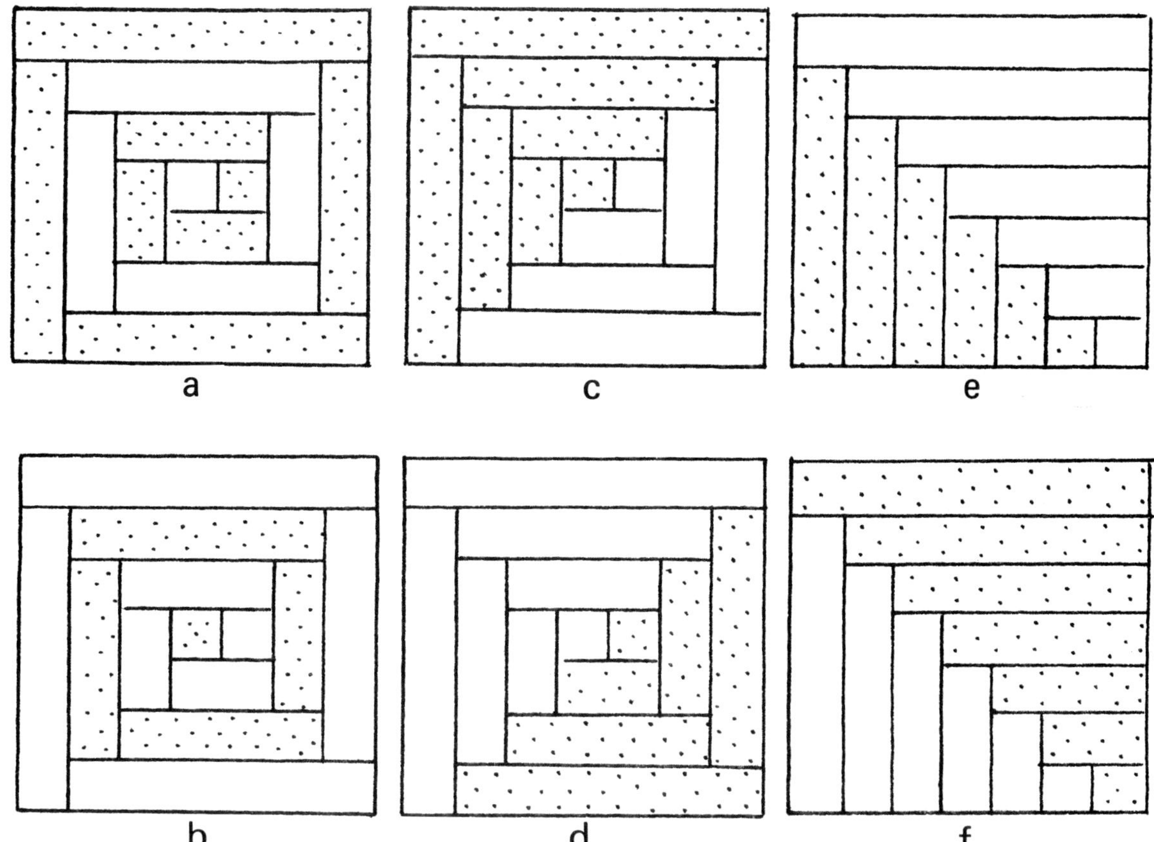

Diagram 45a, b, c, d, e *and* f *Three pairs of positive-negative blocks.*

negative versions of the block design are used. In diagram 45 the three pairs of blocks are of this latter type. The dark areas in diagram 45a are light areas in diagram 45b, thus if diagram 45a is the positive version, diagram 45b is the negative version. The same can be said of the two pairs diagrams 45c and 45d and diagrams 45e and 45f. The significance of using positive and negative blocks to vary the design can be seen in diagram 46.

Conclusion

At the beginning of this chapter, two pre-requisites for exploring Log Cabin patchwork were mentioned. One of these, the use of a suitable technique, has been discussed. The other, familiarity with Log Cabin patchwork, needs further consideration. It is easy to become familiar with the basic blocks by making a small article in traditional style. The next step is to try something slightly different, maybe just a single block. Perhaps this will give you another idea to try. This process of one idea triggering another, leads to the gradual development of a personal design language. Fabrics are never wasted when used in this way. It is important to keep your experimental work where you can see it, as this often provides the stimulus for a new idea.

Sketching is an indispensable tool, enabling you to see the effect of many variations of a design without unnecessary waste of time or fabrics. It is useful to keep all sketches for future reference. Remember though that colouring your sketch with paints or crayons does not give the same effect as using the actual fabrics.

There is a third pre-requisite for designing Log Cabin patchwork, and that is to cultivate a positive attitude to mistakes. No amount of

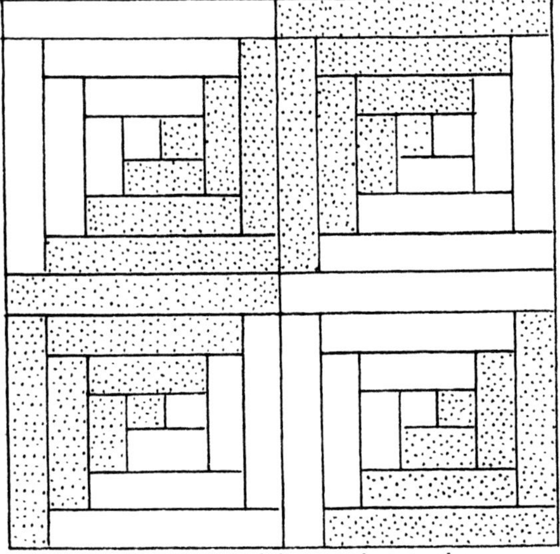

a Blocks positive and negative

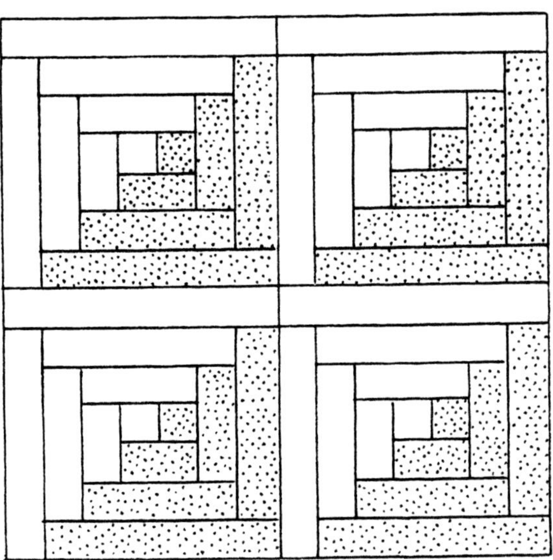

b Blocks all of one type

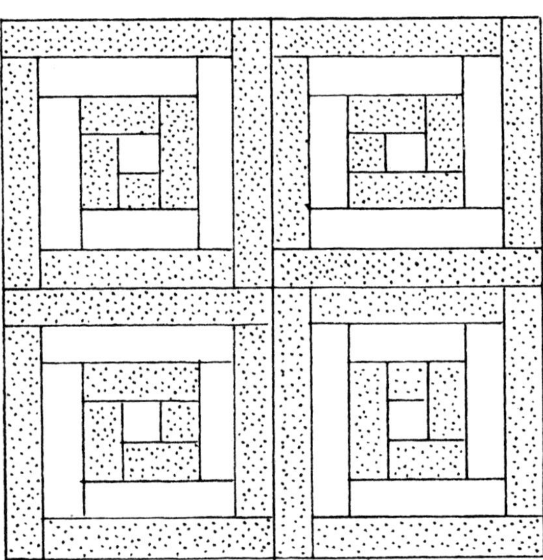

c Blocks all of one type

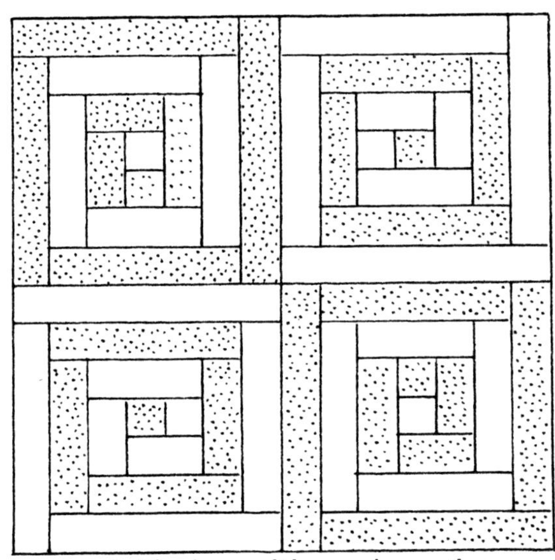

d Blocks positive and negative

Diagram 46a, b, c *and* d *Using positive-negative blocks to vary the design.*

experience can ensure success for every piece of work, as each piece is different from anything attempted previously. Surprises and unexpected effects are inevitable too, and add to the excitement.

All this is really a great opportunity to learn from experience and to discover unimagined possibilities rather than a manifestation of failure. It is what makes the exploration of Log Cabin patchwork an enjoyable and rewarding experience.

For further reading on this topic see the Bibliography on p. 110.

Seminole patchwork

After the Indian wars in the 1880s in America the Seminole Indians in the south-east part of the continent retired to the swampy forests of Florida and remained in almost complete isol-

Figure 46 *Seminole Indian patchwork.*

ation for decades. During that time they developed their own variations of patchwork. They use it largely as trimming on skirts, shawls, etc., although I have seen skirts made entirely of patchwork.

Seminole patchwork is sewn entirely by machine and many strips of material, in a variety of widths and colours, are joined. These are cut across with straight or sloping lines and the pieces joined again. This can be done a number of times making the patterns more and more complex.

The strip in the small bag (*figure 46*) is surprisingly complicated. I purchased it from the Indian Craft Shop in the building of the Department of the Interior in Washington. I was taken to this shop by an Indian woman who had worked in the department and was intensely interested in the heritage and skills of her people (*diagrams 47 and 48*).

By stitching just below the edge of the final arrangement of the patches another distraction has been introduced to cause more variety. Rows of ric-rac braid have also been used as decoration on this bag. It is of bright red cotton fabric with small amounts of bright green and white and the base is basketry made of grasses. It is only $4\frac{1}{2}$ in. (11·25 cm) deep and 13 in. (32·5 cm) around (*colour plate 6*).

String patchwork

This form of patchwork has similarities to Log Cabin patchwork in that it is made with many straight strips of material machined to a backing. In this case the backing is the interlining and, therefore, has the interlining in place before the lining is attached.

The coloured strips are folded and pressed, then placed and machined, as in Log Cabin, with the stitching in the fold of the strip. Then the strip is folded back over the stitching. The next strip covers the rough edges of the previous row.

When successive blocks are placed side by side on the backing in this method they abut each other and, to complete a quilt, for instance, a grid of strips is then machined over the joins. These covering strips may be either plain or patterned but will all be of the same material.

Rows of machine stitching are now made as close as possible to the joins of the strips in the blocks, through all layers (known as 'ditch-stitching' in the U.S.A.). These rows may be sewn in a colour which matches or contrasts with the lining. The lining may be plain or patterned.

To use this method for clothes (*figure 47*), the wadding would have been cut out to a garment pattern and the pattern of strips worked out to fit into the shapes of the garment pieces. These would be sewn in place before the lining could be set in. The stitching would then be done through all layers.

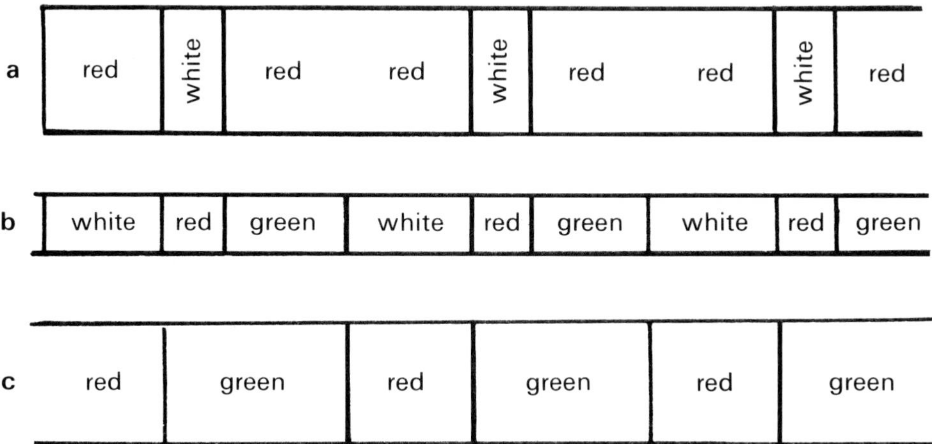

Diagram 47a, b *and* c *Simple strips of patchwork which are cut across in Seminole patchwork.*

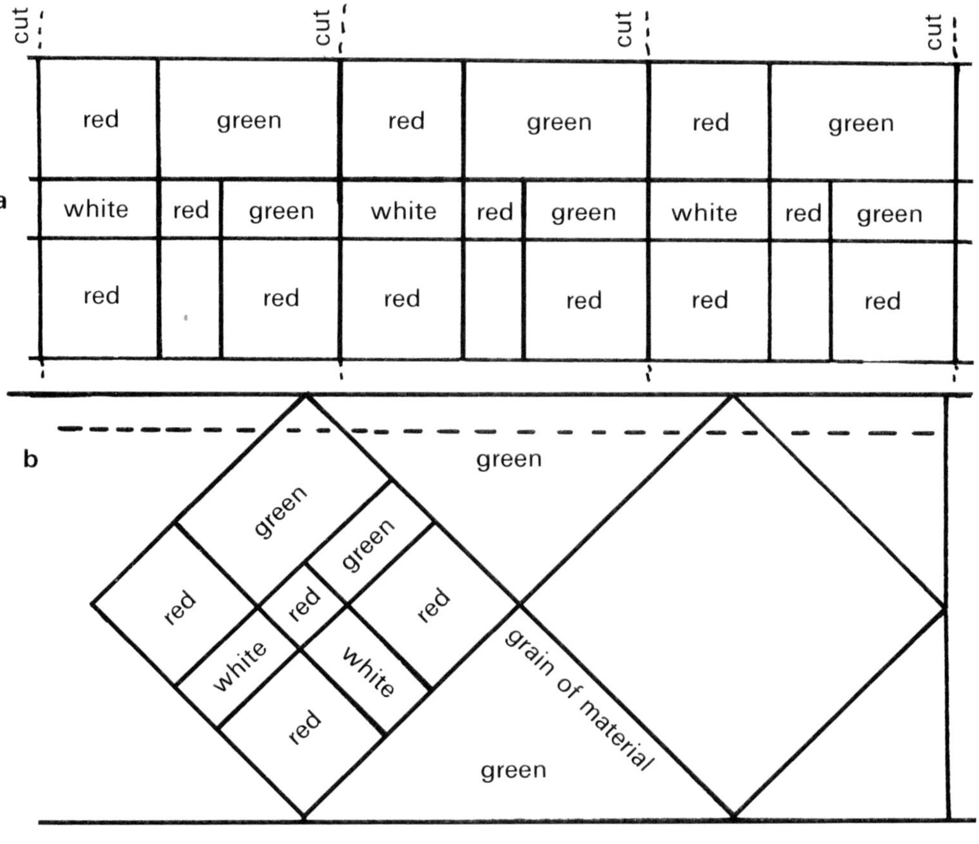

Diagram 48a *and* b *Pieces re-joined to make complicated patterns in Seminole patchwork.*

Figure 47 *String patchwork waistcoats.*

In a garment there will be seams which must be neatened by hand, or the lining made before it is set within the outer shell.

In the waistcoats figure 47a has a central motif made in traditional Log Cabin manner which is inconspicuous because of the closely patterned fabric which is used; figure 47b has a central motif built up around an example of Seminole patchwork.

Figure 48 *Strip patchwork jacket.*

7 Utilizing patchwork

Quilts

To many patchworkers the technique means quilts and nothing else.

In Colonial American days every girl was supposed to have made twelve quilts before her marriage. A thirteenth was made by her friends and relatives when she was to be married and this 'Marriage Quilt' was given to her by them although she may have quilted it herself.

The quilts vary greatly in appearance from the very gay ones to the sombre, but very lovely, ones made by the Amish people in America.

This strict sect of protestants came originally from Holland and Switzerland and to this day adhere firmly to simple principles of life and labour. They are farming people who think higher education is not needed and their schooling goes only so far as is necessary to teach them how to farm and raise a family. Their world belongs to the pre-Industrial Revolution in many ways. Today, as in the seventeenth century, the Amish adhere to the principle of nonconformity. They live in the world and yet are not 'of it'. Their clothes are simple and made from plain fabrics using blues, greys, blacks, maroons and purples. The pieces make their quilts. Very occasionally a plain bright colour will add a jewel-like touch to a dark quilt but patterned pieces are never included.

Frances Lichten writes of these people in *Folk Art in Rural Pennsylvania*, and with reference to their quilts she calls them 'artists in salvage', and this title could be applied to all patchworkers who make do with what is to hand in the traditional patchwork way.

Hawaiian quilts, on the other hand, are bright, colourful and striking. They are cut from two pieces of material – both the complete size of the quilt. One layer is white and the other a bright, plain colour. The coloured piece of material is folded in half and then again in half and the design cut out in quadruplicate in the manner of cutting paper shapes in childhood. Nowadays they are usually made in quarters and joined. The designs are based on Hawaiian traditional patterns – the pineapple, the ceremonial plaited palm leaf fans etc. – which were used in local crafts before the advent of the Americans. The patterns are usually placed in the four corners and as a centrepiece. It's more like a fairly extravagant form of appliqué.

The explanation offered to me was that the making of cloth in the islands had been such a laborious undertaking by primitive methods that when bolts of material became available the urge to be expansive was irresistible.

The quilts that I saw were in the Polynesian Cultural Centre, where representative crafts of the various Pacific Islands were displayed. The quilts were folded in plastic bags as the traditional open-sided huts would provide little protection from the weather but the bold designs were clearly visible.

American patchwork was done without using papers. No doubt paper was not readily available in frontier communities. Local conditions

Figure 49 *Sailor's quilt, dating from the nineteenth century, unfinished.* From the Embroiderers' Guild Collection.

play a large part in the crafts of the communities other than those well supplied with more than primary products. The small floral patterns which are a feature of American quilts in the early days were cut from the bags in which dry cereals were packaged.

The papers which have survived in unfinished quilts in England were frequently cut from letters and bills. One quilt I heard of contained papers cut from indent lists showing amounts of spices purchased in 1790.

Before the manufacture of precision-cut templates, the shapes were made by folding paper and cutting with scissors – most were based on a square from which diamonds, triangles, hexagons and octagons could be got.

Two unfinished quilts are in the possession of the Embroiderers' Guild, Victoria, Australia, which were made by a sailor in the days of sailing ships. In one there are an estimated 18,000 pieces in $\frac{1}{4}$ in. (6 mm) hexagons. It measures 26 in. (65 cm) along each side. The fabrics are dated 1835 (*figures 49 and 50*).

Some old quilts are a wonderful source of designs. There is one in the Victoria & Albert Museum, London, made up of a myriad of patterns (*figure 51*). It is like a sampler of patchwork possibilities. I have seen photographs of ones in the USA making use of this idea. There is a slightly different approach evident in a quilt in the collection at Worthing Museum in England. Here, the different combinations of shapes are quite small and applied to plain, pale coloured squares – only about 4 in. (10 cm) pieces. The source could be related to that of the American patchwork.

One thing we learn from these old quilts is that if the maker was short of a patterned piece she did not let that deter her – she embroidered a sprig, or flower, or a bird, or whatever was needed, on a plain piece of material and used that (*figures 36a and b*).

Another thing that becomes obvious is that,

Figure 50 *Detail of* figure 49. *Made of* $\frac{1}{4}$ *in. (6 mm) hexagons.*

Figure 51 *Quilt using a myriad of patterns.* (Reproduced by permission of the Victoria and Albert Museum, London.)

rather than lack a piece, it is permissible to have a join in a patch. This is the lesson of patchwork: waste nothing; use everything.

The quilting in patchwork is an entirely functional process. It holds the different layers together and should not be so conspicuous that it detracts from the patchwork design. Not so in traditional English quilting where the material is plain and the interest is in the stitched design which can be very complex.

As an alternative to quilting, patchwork quilts can be 'tied' or 'tufted'. These are stitches inserted at intervals, tied in a reef knot and the ends cut off leaving a small tuft on the right side of the quilt. This is usually done with coarse Pearl cotton in the same colour as the background material.

Charming nursery quilts can be made from pieces of Viyella or Clydella.

A type of quilt that was a favourite in America is the Friendship quilt made by a group of people who presented it to a departing member of the community. Each member of the working party embroidered her name on the section which she pieced.

This idea of one quilt being executed by a whole community brings to mind a story about a patchwork quilt that was made in Australia.

About 1960 a very diverse group of women found themselves, with their husbands, in a mineral prospecting camp at Thargominda in central Australia. Their points of contact were few but the youngest member, a bride of a few months, wrote to her mother asking her to send her the makings of a patchwork quilt. Shown what to do, the women worked with a will and finished the quilt. The oldest woman in the party could not manage a needle and thread – she had run a trucking business all her life – but she cut the papers.

The group decided that they would present the finished quilt to this woman. They baked a spread, put on their party clothes, held the quilt up and had their photographs taken standing in front of it at their camp in the desert. Then they had their party.

Shortly afterwards camp was moved across the desert. On the way one truck caught fire and on that truck was the quilt. What did the women do? They made another quilt to replace the lost one for the bereft owner!

Preparation for quilting

The Oxford Dictionary's definition of a quilt is 'bed-covering made of padding between two layers of linen', and of a coverlet 'a counterpane or quilt' but it does not say that it must have padding between the layers.

To make your patchwork into a quilt you will need to place it face down on a large flat surface – a table or the floor is the usual solution. Smooth it free from all wrinkles. Lay the padding on top of it. You will probably have to join the padding to get the size. Do this by hand, catching the edges together so that they touch but do not overlap.

Smooth from the centre out and make sure there is no excess amount. Pin around the edges, then tack regularly so it cannot slip.

The next step is to place the lining, which has been joined to make a piece *with turnings* of the correct size to fit the size of the patchwork, and in accordance with your desired method of finishing.

Starting in the centre, pin it up to the top, down to the bottom and from the centre to each side. It is helpful if the centre point on each side of the patchwork and of top and bottom is marked on the quilt and the lining. There is less chance of the work becoming crooked.

Continue pinning, working out from the centre in all directions. When you have all layers firmly pinned together turn the quilt over just to reassure yourself that there will be no puffs or wrinkles on the surface when it is completed.

Now tack through all layers in a grid pattern. This can be done from the right side or the back but if the pins are put in from the back then they will be easier to remove if the tacking is done from the same side.

Quilting or tufting is the next step and you are ready to commence.

Finishing the edge of a quilt

1 To finish the quilt with a *piping* the method is the same as that used to finish a cushion, method 1, steps a, b, and c as described on page 96.

Do this before placing the padding and backing in place. Finally hem the lining to the back of the piping after any quilting or tufting has been done.

2 To finish the quilt with a *plain border* the same as the lining material, make the lining 6 in. (15 cm) larger all around than the quilt. Turn in a hem 3 in. (7·5 cm) wide all around the lining. This hem should be turned on the front of the lining, not the back. Mitre the corners and tack hem and corners carefully. Make sure that when the quilt is assembled joins in the lining and the rough edges of the hem will be hidden between the lining and the patchwork.

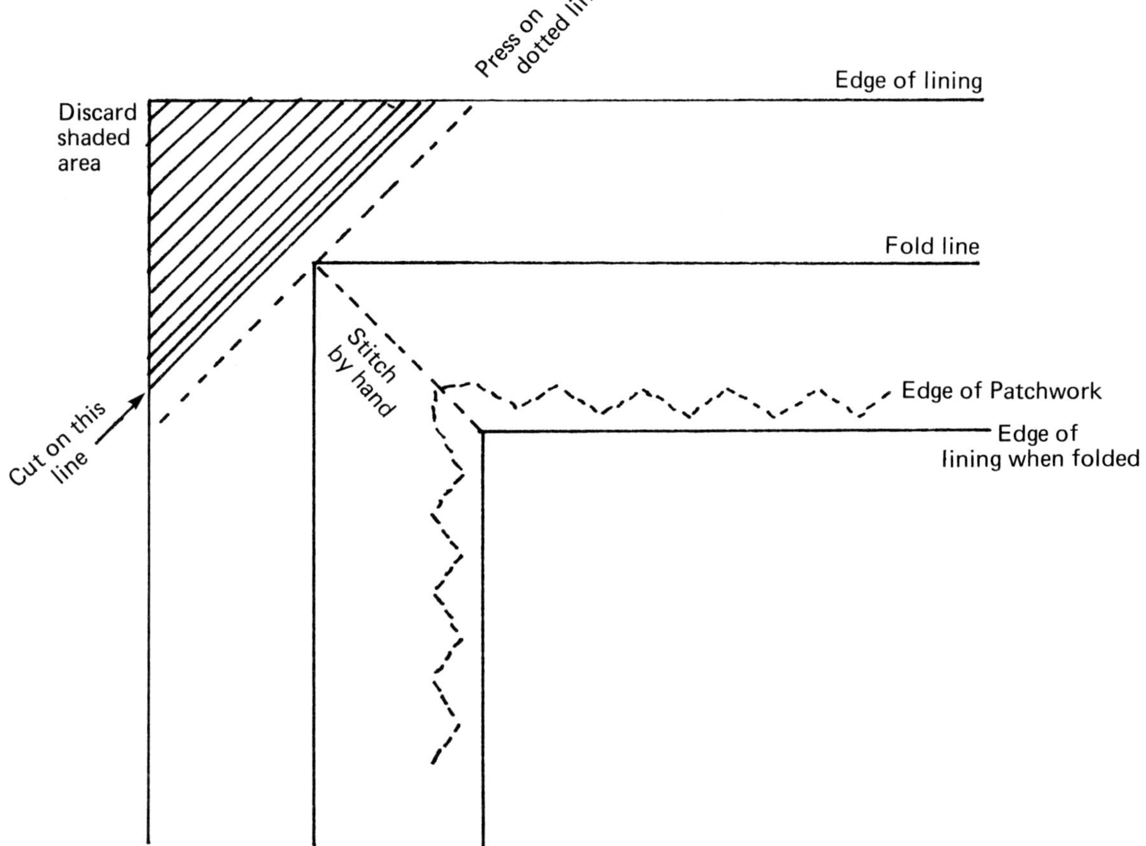

Diagram 49 *One method of mitring a corner and turning the hem of the lining so that it forms a plain border onto which the edge of the patchwork is sewn when making a quilt.*

Finally hem the edges of the patches onto the projecting hem of the lining which gives a border. Do this after any quilting or tufting has been done (*diagram 49*).

Patchwork for ecclesiastical purposes

In recent years, well-known English embroiderer, Beryl Dean has used patchwork effectively as decoration on copes and an altar frontal at Westminster Hospital. Designed and made by her, the latter uses a tile pattern of squares in two sizes and oblongs. She was assisted by Elizabeth Elvin in this project. On the larger squares, silk and metal thread embroidery have been added (*figure 52*).

In 1979, to mark the nine-hundredth anniversary of Winchester Cathedral, a group of English embroiderers including Barbara Siedlicka, Nancy Kimmins and Moyra McNeill made a set of copes with the hoods based on Log Cabin patchwork (*colour plate 8*).

Patchwork can also provide colourful highlights on a larger plain area in this type of work. Edith John of Yorkshire, is well known for her colourful church furnishings. She designed and made the Bible cover in figure 53 and colour plate 5. Laid work and beads have been used to provide detailed embellishment on rectangles of coloured silk.

Patchwork for household use

Later in this book I deal with cushions in some detail but here are other uses to which

Figure 52 *Altar frontal at Westminster Hospital, London. The centre panel is composed of metallic colours, and this is surrounded by dull golds, fawn- and cream-coloured velvets.*

Figure 53 *Bible cover; embroidery on silk patchwork.*

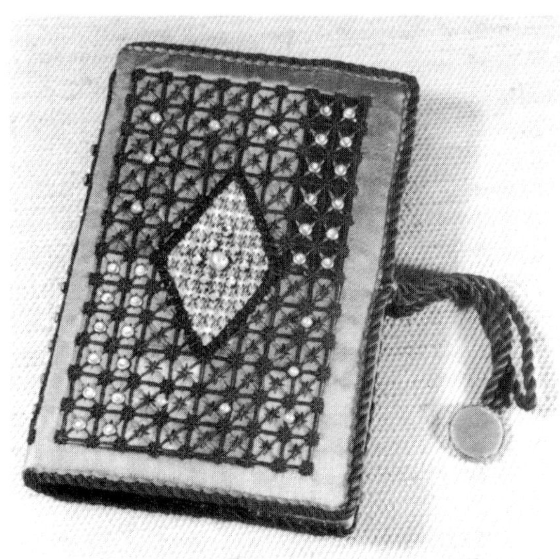

patchwork can be put. Curtains can be entirely made of patchwork or bordered to good effect. Time and patience are the only limitations.

One London embroidress, Gillian Sandilands, won an international embroidery competition with a patchwork tablecloth. Made with hexagons, it fitted a small round table and reached to the floor. The colours, in sections of the circle, varied one from another, and shaded from light at the top of the table to dark at the hem.

Table mats can be easily made. Either pad them with old blanket or foam and then back them, finishing the edge with cording, or neatly oversewing them. Alternatively, make them like an envelope and place a cork mat inside. One set I made were in grey and white striped seersucker with a garland of brightly coloured patches applied. These were made to take a cork mat. They were used very often as they went through the washing machine and needed next to no ironing. A plus mark in a busy household! The table mats and coaster (*figure 54*) were very delicate in colour, being a pearly cream and pale

Figure 54 *Table mat and coaster.*

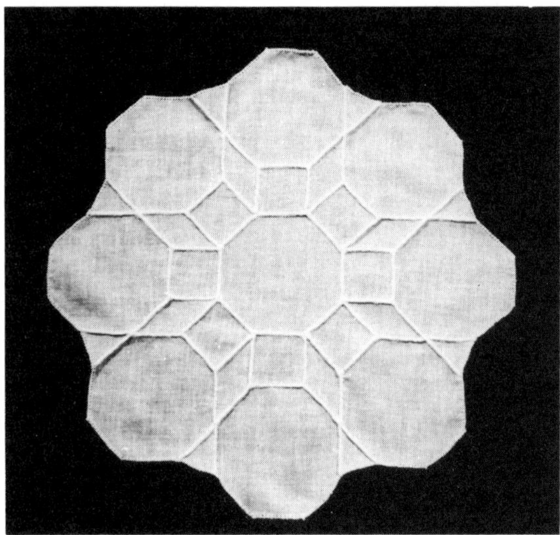

Figure 55 *Fine linen/terylene table mat.*

green. The coasters are reversible with the colours reversed on the two sides.

The mat in figure 55, made from a fine linen/terylene material, looks very fragile. However, it has been through the washing machine a number of times. The patchwork was made in the normal manner and then the seams were trimmed and outlined with double back-stitch to give strength and texture. The seams were cut back closely, one at a time, when the double backstitch was about to be done (*diagram 56*). The edge was finished with a fine binding stitch (*diagram 55*). After completing the stitching, the edges were trimmed right back to the stitching. A few odds and ends appeared after washing and these were trimmed. The hem will not fray back into the stitching.

Figure 56 *Cushion with a cord in the edge. Design based on a shell.*

Figure 57 *'Pineapple' wall hangings in pure silk pieces, quilted and padded.* (See facing page)

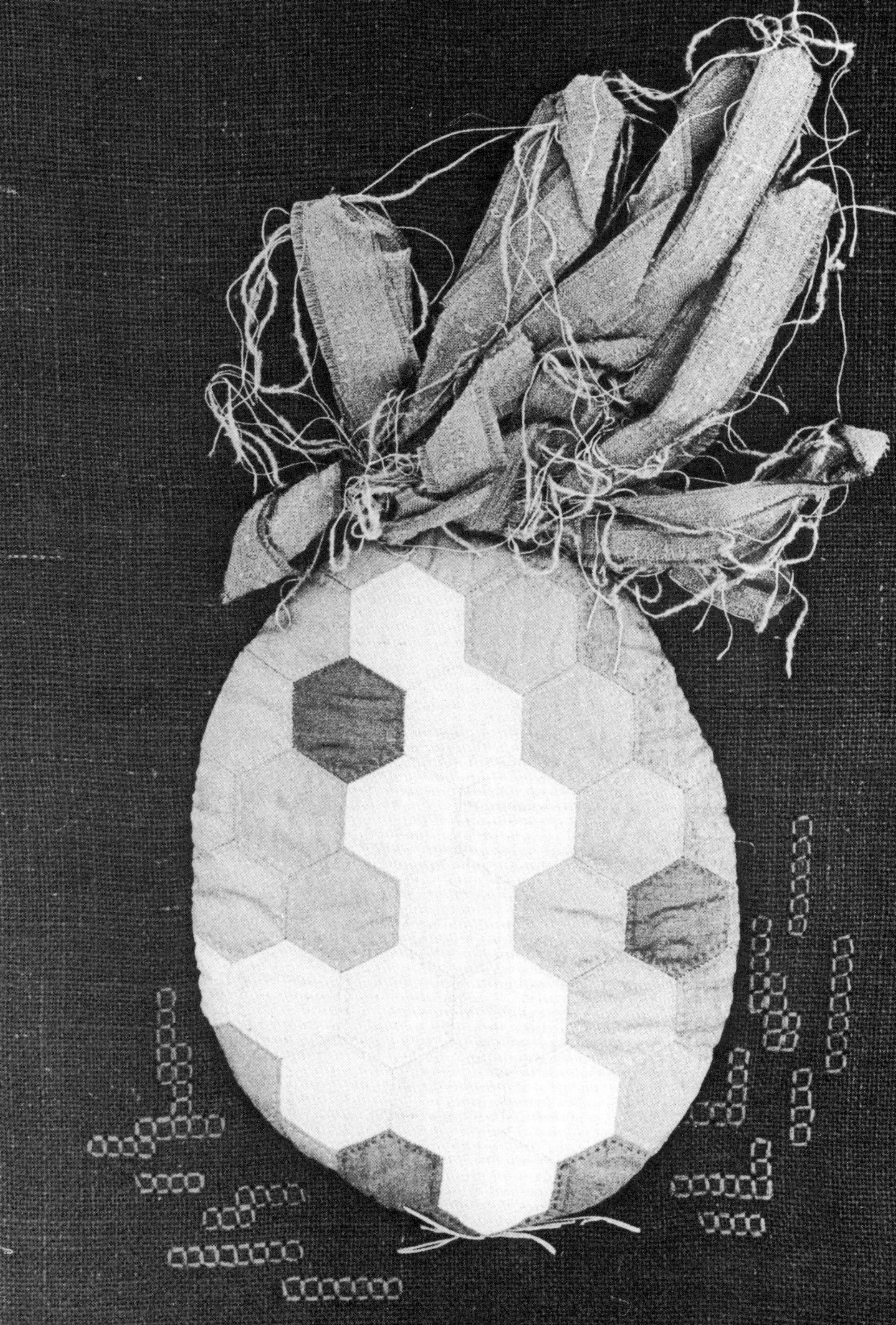

Figure 58 *Black and white fabrics using diamonds and hexagons. The patchwork covers a cardboard container. Two strips of silver kid hide the edge of the patchwork. The 'papers' were left in the patchwork so that the seams would not get out of place as the fabric was eased onto the cardboard cylinder. Then the tackings were removed.*

Figures 56–62 give some idea of the wide range of household articles that can be made using patchwork.

Patchwork for fashion

Patchwork has many uses in the fashion field.

Figure 59 *A beautifully made cushion of tiny floral scraps joined to resemble chintz.*

The quilted jerkin (*figure 63*) would be a welcome addition in après-ski attire. Vogue pattern no. 9561 was used. A crazy patchwork waistcoat made by a friend for her husband used leather pieces in shades from chamois to brown. The bindings and the back were in wool jersey. The pattern was cut in cotton fabric, the pieces were tacked in place and zig-zagged with a sewing machine. Magyar-type jackets are

Figure 60 *Small frilled cushion with well-thought-out medallion in the centre. A scrap of the material is included for extra interest. This cushion is beautifully finished with a frill and piping.*

Figure 61 *Boxes*
Top row from left to right: *fitted work box; square box with floral lining.*
Lower row from left to right: *wooden box with nursery figures inset; round box with star; wooden box with Crazy patchwork inset.*

Figure 62 *Star pincushion from the nineteenth century. It contains 60 hexagon diamonds with cardboard shapes left in the patches. The diamonds are assembled in groups of five and then the stars are joined together.*

Figure 63 *Jerkin showing the separate layers required for quilting. Patchwork applied to background material and some quilting commenced. Ties at the waistline would complete the garment.*

Figure 64 *Two silk berets.*

bright and useful when padded or quilted (*figure 48* on p. 73). Bags in any size, from an evening pochette to a capacious work-bag, look well in patchwork. Small amounts of gay patchwork applied to winter clothing make bright, cheerful accents. Popular and fashionable today are waistcoats made of string patchwork (*figure 47* on p. 73).

Patchwork berets (*figure 64*)

Berets in silk or velvet pieces are attractive. They sit better if quilted and lined.

Vogue pattern no. 9094 is an easy pattern to make and is adaptable to patchwork.

A design based on octagons and its derivatives works into the circular shape well (*figure 64*).

One beret is in sapphire blues and greens. The other one is made in dark brown, cream, black and camel pure silk pieces. The second is a bigger circle and darted at the back. They have a thin layer of wadding which is held in place with quilting to give them body.

Patchwork skirts

Both these skirts are made from a simple A-line skirt pattern.

1 Using hexagons (figure 65a)

Cut the pattern out in paper with only a seam at centre back. Keep this beside you for constant reference.

Make the flower shapes and place them as you wish on the paper pattern, then add the other shapes as necessary. Keep the hexagons flowing as regularly as possible. Eventually, you will certainly have to adjust some shapes at the centre back seam (*figure 65b*).

Hexagon diamonds placed around the flower make a larger size hexagon (*figure 66*). If you use this larger size hexagon for the plain areas in a design like the skirt which is illustrated, it will minimize the work involved. Assembling a skirt in this way becomes a jigsaw puzzle.

If any shaping is required at the waistline try to do it where the patches join and it will be almost impossible to detect it.

Set a zip into a placket at centre back and add a waistband to fit.

Figure 65a *Hexagon skirt (front).*

Figure 65b *Hexagon skirt (back). Where possible in the light areas at the top and the black areas at the bottom enlarged hexagons (as shown in* figure 66*) were used.*

2 *Using graduated diamonds (figure 67)*

Take a simple A-line skirt pattern in your size. Cut it out in paper, with only a seam at centre back.

Fold the skirt in half so that there is a crease at centre front. Fold again, in half and fold, yet again, in half. Crease firmly.

On opening it up you should have seven folded lines and the back edges. Mark the centre fold 0 at the waist and at the hem. Mark from the centre +1, +2, +3, on the fold lines and +4 at the edge. Moving in the other direction mark −1, −2, −3, on fold lines and −4 at the edge. Mark numbers at both waist and hem lines (*diagram 50*).

Now connect with a pencil line +3 at the waist to 0 at the hem. Then connect +2 to −1, +1 to −2, 0 to −3 and −1 to −4. The lines are all sloping in the same direction. Do not try to use the lines which would run off the pattern.

The next step is to connect with pencil lines −4 at the waist to −1 at the hem, −3 to 0 and so

Figure 66 *Building up shapes; the enlarged hexagon.*

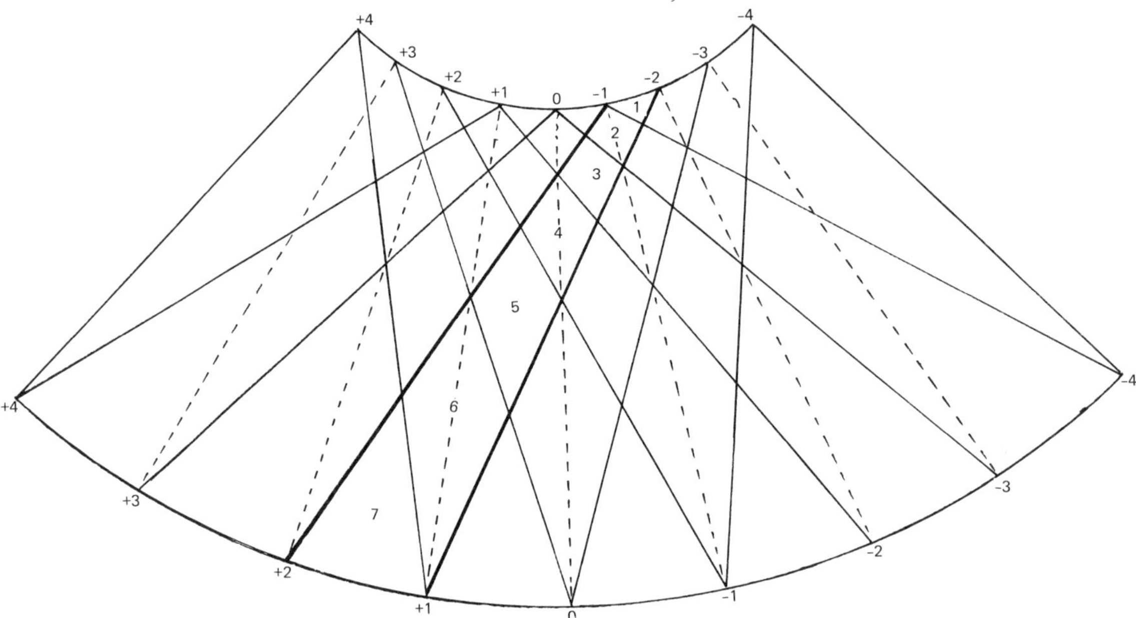

Diagram 50 *How to obtain graduated diamonds when using an A-line skirt pattern. (Dotted lines denote folding in skirt pattern.)*

Figure 67 *Diamond skirt (see* diagram 50*).*

on, drawing lines which slope in the opposite direction.

The centre part of your skirt pattern will now be covered with lines which form diamonds of increasing size from waist to hem. Any one complete strip will contain five full diamonds and two partial diamonds, which if cut out and joined correctly will duplicate this strip. Eight of these strips joined together will make the skirt.

Set the zipper into a diagonal seam. It is easier than cutting into one of the strips. Adjust the waistline and set into a waistband.

The diamonds as cut in paper do not allow for turnings. Allowance for this must be made in cutting the material.

The skirt, as described, is full length. The same method can be used for any length.

Patchwork bags

Circular pouch (*figure 68*)

Make a circular piece of patchwork 36 in. (90 cm) in diameter. Figure 68 commences with a hexagon star in the centre surrounded by hexagons. In this case the sides of the templates measure $1\frac{1}{2}$ in. (3·75 cm). Use the figure as a guide for the placing of your diamonds and hexagons. As the work progresses the number of hexagons needed in each row increases.

When the required size is attained press your patchwork as described on p. 96.

If you decide to have a piping in the edge, cut your work into a smooth edged circle and set the piping in place (see p. 96). If, however, you decide to retain the shaped edges of your patches, carefully tack the edges in place.

Place wadding and lining in place behind the patchwork, tack to keep the layers together and quilt such areas as you think desirable.

To finish the edge cut the wadding carefully to match the outside edge. Cut the lining to have $\frac{1}{2}$ in. (1·25 cm) turnings on every edge. Carefully hem the lining to the patchwork so that it sits quite flat and does not show from the outside. Clip very carefully where needed at the corners.

There are several types of handles that can be used on this type of bag:

Figure 68 *Patchwork for pouch bag showing design, rings in place and plastic hose handle.*

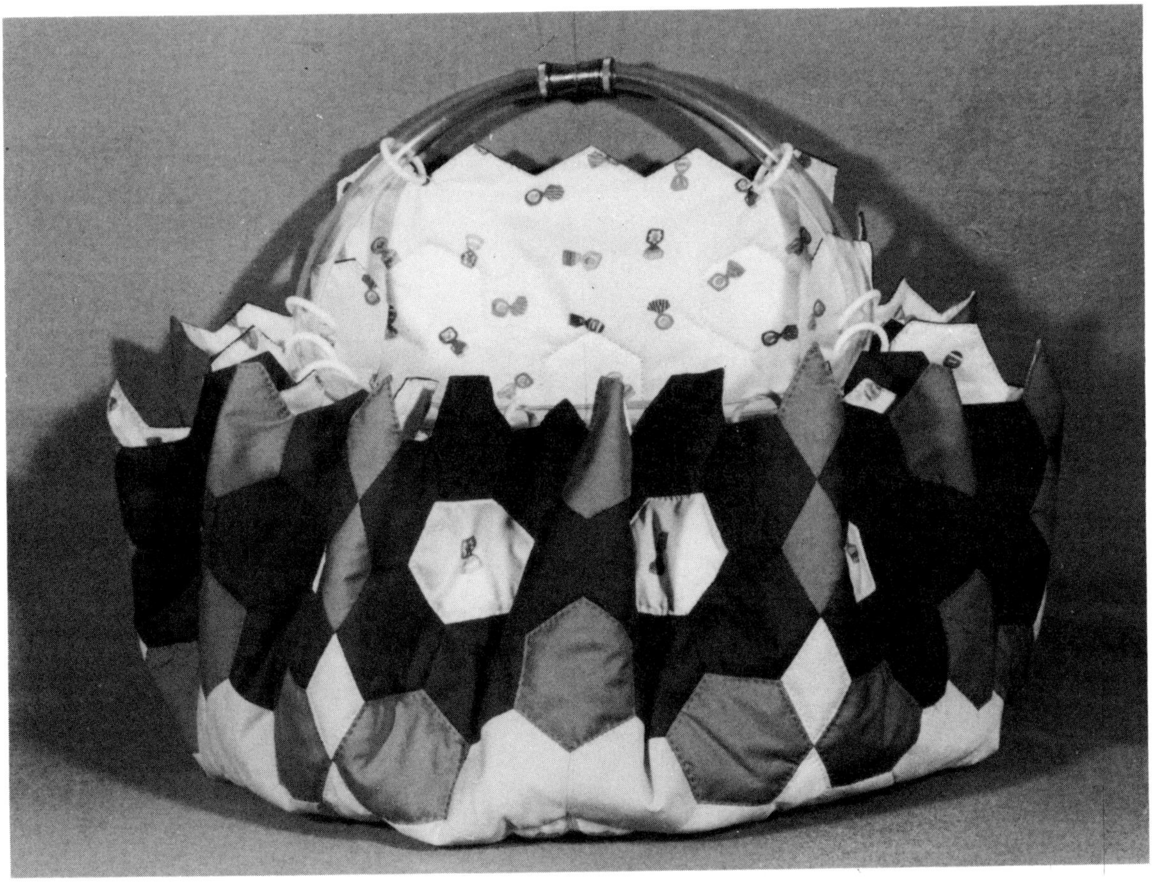

Figure 69 *Completed and assembled pouch bag. Designed and made by the author.*

1 A firm ring of plastic or cane. If using this method the rings which you sew to your bag must be further apart than the diameter of the handle. This is because, when you pick the ring up to carry the bag, the rings on the bag slide to the lower side of the ring over the widest part of the handle.

2 A long strip of fabric which can be hemmed on each side, or folded double, seamed and turned inside out like a belt. It needs to be longer than the outside edge of the circle of the patchwork. Thread it through the rings and tie the ends in a knot. This enables you to lay your bag on the table fully open like a tablecloth with all the contents fully visible.

3 A piece of clear plastic hose joined with the correct size of brass fitting used for joining two pieces of garden hose (*figure 68*). (Lacquer the brass fitting before inserting it into the plastic hose to keep it from becoming dull.)

The plastic hose, strange as it may seem, is a very comfortable handle. It can be long enough so that, when resting on the table, it is large enough to see what is inside easily but, being pliable, it changes shape when picked up and allows the rings on the bag to slide easily from one position to the other without trouble. It makes a handle that rests comfortably on the shoulder for carrying. 1 yard or 1 metre is a convenient size.

For the rings on the bag use plastic curtain rings which open. They are easily manipulated when you wish to take the bag off the handle for cleaning. Or you can have several different bags for the one handle. Eight to twelve rings are sufficient on a bag of this size. Sew the rings at a regular distance from each other. In figure 69 the rings have been carefully placed so that the radiating diamonds show on the edges of some of the folds when the bag is being carried.

A chatelaine attached to one of the rings would be an appropriate addition that would turn this pouch into a capacious work bag.

The chatelaine (*figure 70*)

There are three items involved in this unit (*figure 70*).

The pincushion: The base of the pincushion is a $\frac{3}{4}$ in. (1·85 cm) hexagon plus six strips which are $2\frac{1}{4}$ in. (6·85 cm) long by $1\frac{1}{4}$ in. (3 cm) wide at one end and tapered at the other. Sew one strip to each side of the hexagon and each to its neighbour making a conical shape. Leave an opening at the top just large enough to turn it inside out and stuff.

There is a bag made of crochet that fits over this point to hold a thimble. Make a circle in chain that will fit around the pointed end of the pincushion about $\frac{1}{2}$ in. (1·25 cm) from the top. The example in the illustration is made in no. 40 sewing cotton in a colour to match the patchwork. Round 2 and subsequent rounds of crochet can be chain stitch loops into the previous row.

The bag must be loose enough to hold the thimble comfortably. A draw string should be threaded through the final row of crochet.

Sew the bag to the pincushion. The thimble sits on the point of the pincushion inside the crochet bag.

The scissors' case: this is made in the shape of a triangle just large enough to hold comfortably your embroidery scissors. Shape the top into a pleasing scallop.

Cut this shape, twice, in light-weight cardboard. Cut the lining material and the outside fabric $\frac{1}{4}$ in. (6 mm) larger than the cardboard.

Place each cardboard shape on a piece of outer material. Clip edges, carefully, where necessary to make them turn over the cardboard shapes. Glue in place. Use glue sparingly. Leave to dry.

Turn seam allowance on lining pieces and press flat. (The edges must not project beyond the edges of the cardboard.) Clip material where necessary for a flat fit.

Glue or stitch to inside of the two pieces of fabric covered card. If glued, allow to dry.

Sew the two shapes together along the straight edges placing a bead between every stitch. Then continue sewing beads to each curved edge, separately, in the same way. If the stitches are too close together the beads will not lie flat.

A loop on one side of the top opening and cord on the other side that is threaded through this loop keeps it closed. Make sure that the cord is long enough to allow you to insert and withdraw the scissors.

Figure 70 *Chatelaine; needle-book, scissors case and pincushion with thimble bag.*

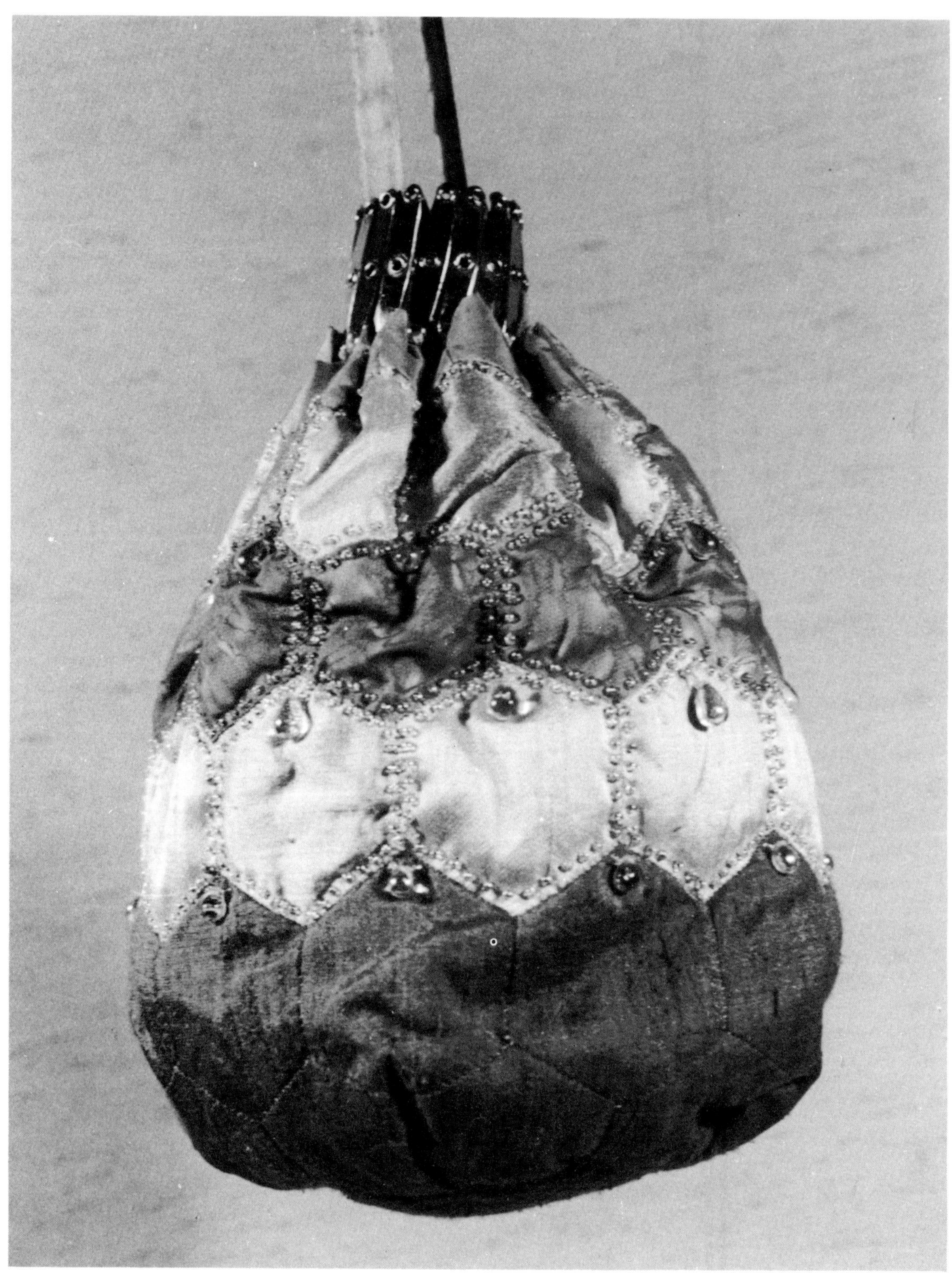

Figure 71 *Bag on an expanding mount.*

In figure 70 a simple design of tiny hexagons was applied to the fabric covering the cardboard before being set in place.

The needlebook: for the front of the needlebook make a piece of patchwork, large enough to cover a piece of cardboard $2\frac{1}{4} \times 4\frac{1}{4}$ in. ($6{\cdot}25 \times 11{\cdot}25$ cm) using small hexagons.

In this case two layers of thin cardboard were cut for both front and back covers. Use the patchwork and one piece of plain material for the front and two pieces of plain material for the back.

On the back of the needlebook is a pocket that holds a tape measure. This was placed on the outer material before it was glued to the relevant piece of cardboard.

The material was cut $\frac{1}{4}$ in. (6 mm) larger than each piece of cardboard and the materials glued over the edges of the cards. Then two cards were sewn together for front and back. Using matching thread oversew while placing a small bead on the thread between each stitch.

A hinge was made with buttonhole loops – a loop at each end and one in the middle. A large bead and a loop fasten the book at the lower edge. Flannel pages are sewn inside the covers to hold the needles.

These three items are attached by fine cords to a large bead. The actual knot holding them together is covered with similar beads to those on the edge of the articles and on the crocheted bag for the thimble.

You can add a loop which is large enough to hang on a belt, if you wish, or attach it to the inside of your work bag in any way that is suitable.

Bag with an expanding mount (*figure 71*)
This is a simple bag also made with hexagon patchwork (*figure 71*).

Materials required: 1 piece of hexagon patchwork; 1 piece of lining material; 1 piece of interlining material. (Only needed if outer is very soft silk. In that case soft cotton, linen or calico may be used.)

Open mount to its fullest stretch and measure around it. Make a patchwork piece exactly this size. In the illustration there were ten 1 in. (2·5 cm) hexagons per round. Make it as deep as you wish it to be. Be sure that the pattern will join correctly.

Divide the bottom edge into five equal parts and mark these points. Make a V tuck joining the sloping edges of adjacent patches at these points. Cut a base with sides the length of the distance between the V tucks. Allow good turnings on the fabric base. Join base to the bag on the wrong side.

Make a lining exactly the same size as the bag. Insert lining into bag and overcast top edges together. Attach to mount.

Sew handle, made from a strip of fabric, at two opposite points inside the mount.

8 Finishing patchwork

You have made your piece of patchwork. It is a flat piece. Lay it *face up* on your ironing board or table and remove all the tackings. *Do not* touch the papers which will be underneath. Press carefully.

Now shake your work and most of the papers will fall out. Gently using a fingernail will dislodge any papers that are left.

By doing it this way your papers act as a cushion during pressing and the ridges formed by the turnings do not come through to the surface.

That is why, in Chapter 1, I said 'Have the knots on the right side of flat work.' You can easily remove the tackings. I find a coarse plastic knitting needle is a great help when taking out the tackings.

If, however, you have made pincushions or cushions that must be joined around the edges on the *wrong side* and then turned right side out, you need the knots on the back for easy removal.

The edges of quilts can be finished with a piping if you have planned your pattern to have a straight edge, or the edges of the patches can be hemmed down onto a contrasting border which may be the lining. This is so where you wish to have an edge which shows the outline of your patches.

In making bags, if the patches can be designed to fit into each other at the sides instead of being seamed in the usual way, it is a point-winning detail.

There are various methods of finishing cushions which are detailed below.

Method 1: Cushion with piping

(*figure 21 on p. 34*)

Do this in three stages.

a Cut a bias strip so that when the cord is inserted between the folded material there will be $\frac{1}{2}$ in. (1·25 cm) seam allowance, and make the piping 3 in. (7·5 cm) longer than the measurement around the cushion. This measurement is taken $\frac{1}{2}$ in. (1·25 cm) inside the edge of the cushion. If the bias strip needs to be joined, this is sewn on the grain of the material. Be sure the cord has been shrunk. Just soak it in cold water and hang to dry.

b With matching cotton, machine close to the cord. Use a zipper foot for this line of machining (*diagrams 51a* and *51b*).

c Tack the piping all around the edge of the front of the cushion, on the right side of the patchwork. The raw edges of the piping and the edges of the cushion should match. Clip the piping to $\frac{1}{16}$ in. (1·5 mm) from the stitching line at the corners. The fabric will open out to allow the piping to sit flat. There must be no fullness in the piping.

To avoid having corners that stick out like ears, mark a point $\frac{3}{4}$ in. (1·85 cm) in from the corners and slope the edges in towards this mark. Start the slope $2\frac{1}{2}$ in. (6·25 cm) on either side of the corner. Do not 'round' the corners, just bring the corners in and slope the edges (*diagram 52*).

Where the ends of the piping meet pull cord out and cut back enough so that the material overlaps but there is no bulk of the overlapping

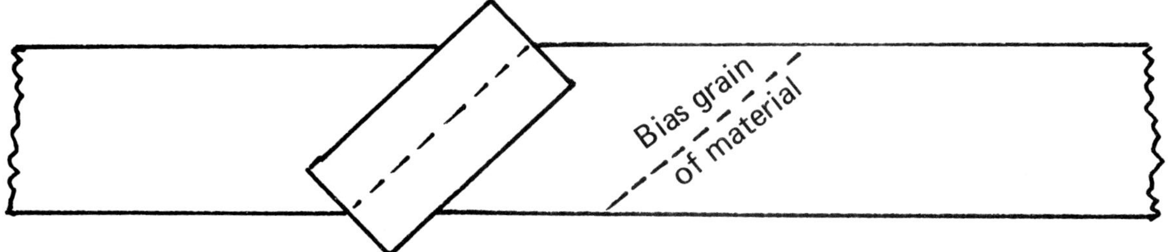

Diagram 51a *A strip of bias fabric with a join on the fabric grain.*

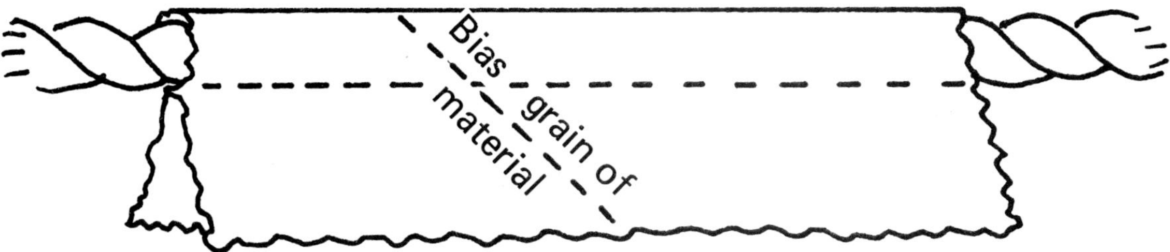

Diagram 51b *How to make a piping.*

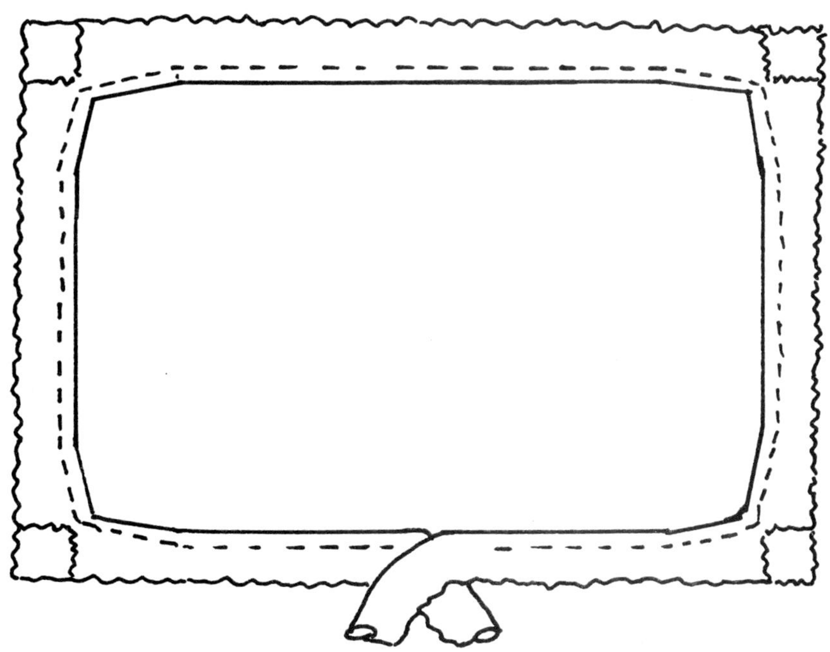

Diagram 52 *One piece of a cushion with piping stitched in place and corners clipped to sit flat. Corners are shaped so that they will not stick out like ears.*

cord. Allow the cord to run back inside casing and bring piping down at an angle.

Stitch a second time on the same line as the stitching of the piping. Use matching thread.

Now place the back of the cushion over the front – right sides facing – and tack around the edges. Stitch on previous stitching line. Be sure to leave an opening so you can turn it inside out.

Cut away a small triangle of material at each corner to eliminate as much bulk as possible at the corners.

Turn the cushion inside out and pull the corners into place. Place the cushion pad inside or fill with stuffing.

Method 2: cushion with a wall

(*figure 17 on p. 31*)

You usually want to make a cushion in this manner when the insert is sponge rubber or plastic foam.

Have the foam cut $\frac{3}{4}$ in. (1·85 cm) larger than your finished cushion size. Sew a piping around your cushion top and bottom. The 'wall' is a straight strip of desired width – usually $1\frac{1}{2}$–3 in. (3·75–7·5 cm) wide and long enough to fit around the cushion plus 1 in. (2·5 cm) for joining.

Tack one edge of the strip to the cushion top and the other edge to the bottom of the cushion. There must be no fullness in the strip. Join the ends of the strip. The corners must match on both sides of the 'wall'.

Stitch strip to cushion. Leave part of one side open to insert cushion pad. Turn cushion inside out. Insert cushion pad. Close remaining part of seam by hand.

If your cushion cover must be removable for washing you can insert a zipper in the 'wall'. Do this before inserting the 'wall' in the rest of the cushion (*see p. 99* and *diagram 54b*).

Method 3: Cushion with design carried down the sides (*figure 32 on p. 41*)

Sometimes with patchwork your pattern can carry over the edge so that filled with a foam pad instead of inserting a strip you can mitre the corners of the patchwork top and allow the pattern to continue, thus making the sides. Then join the sides to the back. The foam pad should be $\frac{3}{4}$ in. (1·85 cm) larger than the finished measurement of the cushion so your patchwork must include the depth of the pad plus seam allowance on all sides (*diagram 53*).

To insert a zipper

In the back of a cushion

Insert the zipper before joining the front to the back (*diagram 54a*).

Cut the material for the back of your cushion $1\frac{1}{2}$ in. (3·75 cm) longer than the front but the same width. Cut it in half across the width and press $\frac{3}{4}$ in. (1·85 cm) hem on each piece across the width. Insert the zipper with the two hems completely hiding it. Place one folded edge so that it hides the teeth and stitch behind the line of the teeth. Place the other folded edge so that it is just below the teeth. Stitch this edge as close to the fold as possible. Material must never be stretched onto a zipper. Fullness of $\frac{1}{2}$ in. (1·25 cm) in 12 in. (30 cm) makes a perfect setting. With this method the zipper is hidden.

In the side of a cushion

In this case insert the zipper into the 'wall' before joining the 'wall' to the cushion (*diagram 54b*).

Draw a pencil line where you wish to place the zipper. The line should be 1 in. (2·5 cm) longer than the tooth area of your zipper. Cut along this line, stopping $\frac{1}{2}$ in. (1·25 cm) from the ends. Clip on an angle, on both sides at both ends of this line so that you can turn a narrow hem all around this area. Lay opening over the zipper and tack and then stitch around edge as close to the edge as possible. With this method the zipper shows.

To bond fabrics

Cut a piece of Bondina or Viledon the size of the materials to be bonded. Do not remove the supporting paper.

Lay one piece of material on your ironing board or table, face down. Cover with bonding web. Make sure it does not extend beyond the

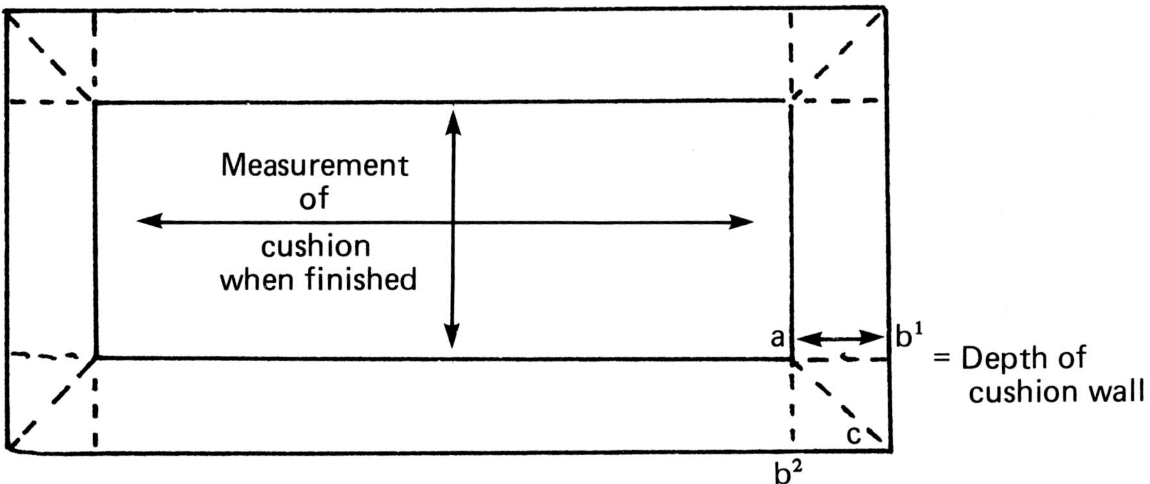

Diagram 53 *One piece of a cushion with corners marked for mitring to make a 'wall'. Fold corner on line a–c. Bring a–b¹ to a–b². Machine on line a–b. Repeat with other corners.*

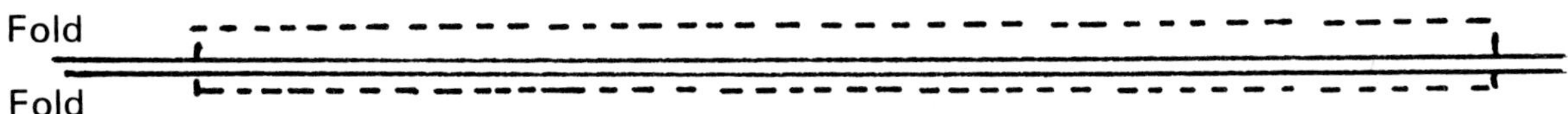

Diagram 54a *Method of inserting a zip so that it is hidden.*

Diagram 54b *Method of inserting a zip so that it shows.*

edges of fabric because when heat is applied it will adhere to the cover of the board or table. Remove the paper. Carefully lay the other piece of material on top without moving the bonding web.

Press with as hot an iron as the fabric will take. Never use steam for this process.

To make a cord (*figure 72*)

Cotton in matching colour to the patchwork is needed to make a cord.

Each strand needs to be two and a half times the desired finished length. Cut as many strands as needed to make the finished cord as thick as you wish. Knot the ends.

Two people, each holding a pencil in the ends of the strands, make a cord quickly and easily. Each person spins the pencil in a clockwise direction until the strands will not twist any tighter. It helps to hold the strands loosely between thumb and forefinger of the hand which is not holding the pencil. Hold the strands close to where the pencil is.

When the strands are very tightly twisted, place a weight on the middle of the cord and bring the two ends together. The weight will help the cord to twist evenly. (A cup hook screwed into the hole through a small lead fishing sinker is excellent for the purpose.)

Figure 72 *Steps in making a cord and a tassel.*

Fasten the ends of the cord securely. Sometimes you can hide these ends inside your work but sometimes it is convenient to knot the ends and use the knot as the basis for an ornamental tassel (*figure 72*).

The head of a tassel can be covered with detached buttonhole stitch. It is easiest, though not the traditional way, to make the first row of buttonhole stitches into the tight threads which hold the tassel together and then work towards the cord.

Beading can be added to the head of a tassel to make it more important! Some beautiful ones had complicated macramé work on them or even numbers of smaller ones hanging from them in examples from the nineteenth century.

I have not been able to cover all aspects of patchwork in the preceding pages, but I hope that the patterns, photographs and hints for working, accumulated over many years, will show you what a versatile craft it is and will inspire you to carry out your own adaptations and ideas.

Appendix I: Stitches used in patchwork

Binding stitch An inconspicuous edging stitch used where a neat finish is required as on a transparent table mat.

Follow diagram 55. Turn a tiny hem and tack it.

The needle travels from:

a–b twice; these are buttonhole stitches.
a–c (behind the material)
c–b
b–c
c–b
b–d (behind the material)
d–c twice; these are buttonhole stitches as at a–b.

Repeat as often as necessary. Fit your stitches as you turn corners and trim any unwanted ends and fabric when the binding stitch is completed.

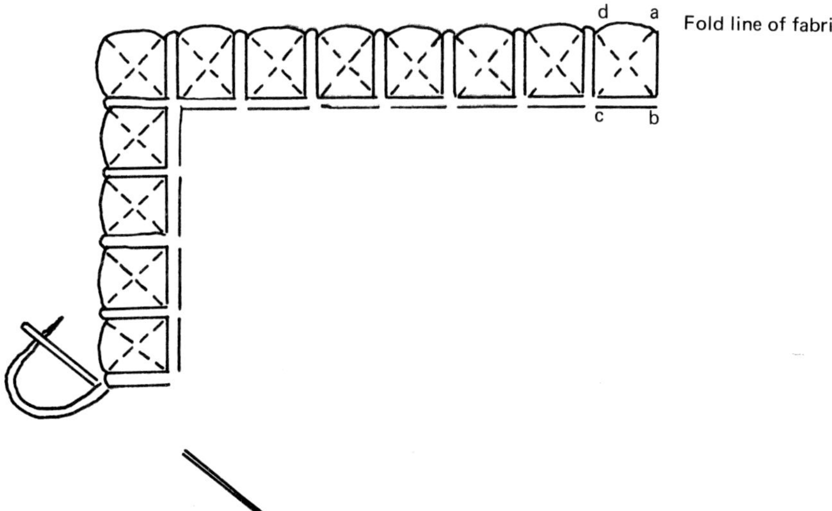

Diagram 55 *Binding stitch.*

Double backstitch

This is the reverse side of herringbone stitch (*see below*). The crossing threads on the back of the material give depth and contrast of tone. When worked behind a closely trimmed seam the stitches give strength to the seam. Each stitch moves from left to right, but work in total progresses from right to left.

Follow diagram 56.

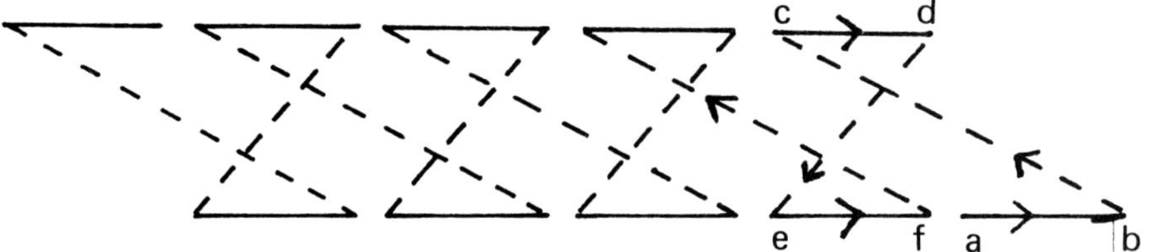

Diagram 56 *Double backstitch.*

Feather stitch

An ornamental stitch allied to buttonhole stitch and frequently used to cover the raw edges of patches in Crazy patchwork.

Follow diagram 57.

Diagram 57 *Feather stitch.*

Gather stitch or gathering

Small stitches similar to running stitch, worked with a strong, fine thread or ordinary sewing cotton used double, so that it does not break when the thread is pulled to form gathers in the material.

Follow diagram 58.

Diagram 58 *Gather stitch.*

Glove stitch

Two separate stitches are required to complete this stitch which has the same purpose as over-casting (*see below*).

One stitch is straight and returns to the same hole as it started from; then the second stitch moves on to be in position to make the first part of the next stitch, so that there is a straight stitch and a slanting one alternately wrapping over the edge.

Follow diagram 59.

Diagram 59 *Glove stitch.*

Hemming

Small slanting stitches which are used to hold the edge of a fold firmly to the main body of the material.

Follow diagram 60.

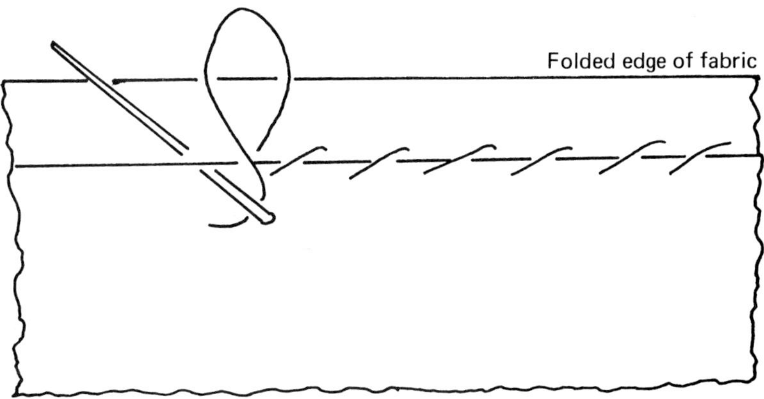

Diagram 60 *Hemming.*

Herringbone

An ornamental stitch worked so that the greater part of the stitch is on the surface of the material. Frequently used to cover the raw edges of patches in Crazy patchwork.

Follow diagram 61.

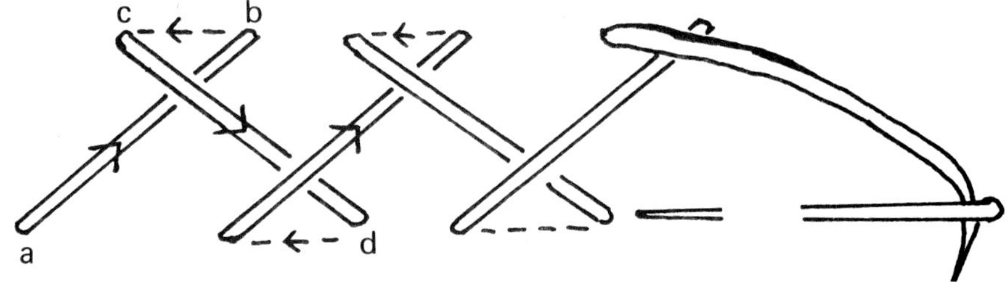

Diagram 61 *Herringbone.*

Overcasting or **oversewing**

Small stitches which hold two pieces of material together by wrapping stitches over the edges.

Follow diagram 62.

Diagram 62 *Overcasting.*

Quilting

Running stitches (which may be stabbed back and forth for convenience in this context) which hold the layers of a quilt together. In patchwork, the stitched designs are usually kept simple.

Follow diagram 63.

Diagram 63 *Running stitch used to join materials together. (Also used to hold layers of fabric together in quilting.)*

Running stitch

Small regular stitches which are the same length on both sides of the fabric. Used for joining materials.

Follow diagram 63.

Slip stitch

This stitch has a family similarity to hemming. It is used to hold a hem in place when it is important that little stitch shows. A very small stitch is taken into the body of the material and then the needle slides through the hem out of sight until it is time for it to emerge and take another tiny stitch into the background.

Follow diagram 64.

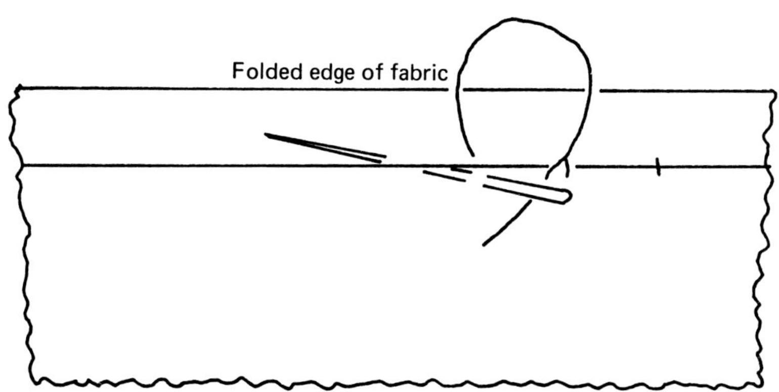

Diagram 64 *Slip stitch.*

Tacking stitch (U.S. **basting stitch)**

A longer stitch but similar to running stitch (*see above*), also left looser and frequently longer on the surface of the material than underneath it. Used to hold materials together temporarily.

Follow diagram 65.

Diagram 65 *Tacking stitch.*

Appendix II: Terms used in patchwork

Bias or **Bias strip** — When fabric is cut so that the grain is neither horizontal nor vertical but at an angle of 45 degrees to the rest of the material.

Coverlet — A covering for a bed or a cot that has no wadding between the outer layers.

Filling — Loose stuffing for giving shape to toys, cushions and pincushions. Resembles cotton wool and is bought by weight. It is usually of man-made fibres nowadays, and thus is fully washable.

Grain of material — The direction of the warp and weft threads.

Mitred corners — Where a hem has been turned around a quilt or a cloth and some of the material cut away to provide a flat, square outline at the corner.

Needles — Sharps: medium length, straight needles with round eyes.

Crewels: medium length, straight needles with oval eyes.

Betweens: shorter than either of the above with round eyes.

All come in a range of sizes – the larger the number the finer the needle. 9s are a satisfactory size for patchwork but use the finest ones you can thread.

Papers or **cards** — Shapes cut in paper using the template as a pattern.

Patches Pieces of material cut using the template as a pattern but plus seam allowances.

Piping The edging used on bedspreads and cushions made of a cord inside a strip of bias material and placed so that it gives a corded edge to the finished article. Can be in a contrasting colour or matching the article.

Quilt A covering for a bed or a cot which has a layer of wadding between two outer layers.

Quilting The stitching which holds the various layers of a quilt together. Can be hand- or machine-sewn.

Sheen The light reflected from material which varies with the direction of the woven threads in the material.

Also a trade name of some mercerized cotton.

Template An accurate shape cut in metal or plastic.

Tile or **block** Several patches joined to make a unit, usually a square.

Or a patchwork design mounted on a square of material, later to be joined to other tiles.

Thread Usually ordinary machine sewing thread on a reel. Coarse embroidery thread, e.g. Broder or Pearl, for ornamental stitching or tufting.

Tufting A method of holding the layers of a quilt together when quilting is not done. A double thread of pearl cotton is taken through the layers twice and then tied in a reef knot and cut off leaving a small tuft of thread on the right side of the quilt.

Wadding or **batting** An airy material used to give warmth and thickness to quilts. Usually of man-made fibres. Can be bought by the yard.

Wall A strip of material sewn around a cushion or pin-cushion to give a straight side rather than a flatter or rounded edge.

Appendix III: Summary of do's and don'ts

Do wash and iron all materials before using.

Do cut papers accurately.

Do cut papers with print parallel to one edge of squares, hexagons and octagons.

Do cut patches on grain of fabric.

Do place papers with printed lines to match grain of fabric.

Do use a short, fine needle.

Do use short lengths of sewing thread.

Do wax the thread.

Do use materials of similar weight.

Do plan work so that it can be done in sections.

Do begin with basic shapes and graduate to complicated ones.

Don't mix cottons and synthetic fabrics.

Don't use synthetic sewing thread except with synthetic materials.

Don't skimp turnings.

Don't let your stitches penetrate the edges of the papers when joining patches.

Don't cut into your material extravagantly.

Don't throw away papers until they are worn out.

List of suppliers

Commercially cut templates are normally available from craft shops and department stores handling embroidery or patchwork supplies. Wax is obtainable from craft shops and tailor's suppliers. Fabrics, threads and accessories are available from drapery stores and from a wide range of department stores. The following have a particularly wide selection.

Great Britain

John Lewis & Company Limited
Oxford Street, London W1A 1EX
(and all branches of the John Lewis Partnership)

Liberty and Company Limited
Regent Street, London W1R 6BA

U.S.A.

Baltazor, Inc.
3262 Severn Avenue
Metairie, LA 70002

Chaparral
3733 Westheimer – Suite 7
Houston, TX 77027

Frederick J. Fawcett
129 South Street
Boston, MA 02130

Happy Hands
3007 S.W. Marshall
Pendleton, OR 97108

Lace Place de Belgique
800 S.W. 17th Street
Beca Reton, FL 33432

Lacis
Antique Lace & Textiles
2150 Stuart Street
Berkeley, CA 97705

Robin & Russ Handweavers
533 N. Adam Street
McMinnville, OR 97128

Robin's Bobbins
Rte. 1 – Box 294A
Mineral Bluff, GA 30559

Rue de France
77 Thames Street
Newport, RI 02840

Van Sciver Bobbin Lace Supply
310 Aurora Street
Ithaca, N.Y. 14850

The Unique and Art Lace Cleaners
5926 Delmar Boulevard
St. Louis. MO 63112

The World in Stitches
82 South Street
Milford. N. H. 03055

Or your local bookseller

Bibliography

Bishop, R. and Safanda, E., *A Gallery of Amish Quilts*, E. P. Dutton & Co. Inc.

Burn, E., *Quilt in a Day* (Log Cabin Pattern), Carlsbad, California, 1979

Colby, A., *Patchwork*, B. T. Batsford Ltd., 1958

Green, S., *Patchwork for Beginners*, Studio Vista, 1971

Gutcheon, E., *The Perfect Patchwork Primer*, Penguin Books

Harding, V., *Patchwork*, Search Press, 1978

James, M., *The Quiltmaker's Handbook*, Prentice-Hall Inc., 1978

James, M., *The Second Quiltmaker's Handbook*, Prentice-Hall Inc., 1981

Ickis, M., *The Standard Book of Quilt making & Collecting*, Dover, 1959

Leman, B. and Martin, J., *Log Cabin Quilts*, Moon over the Mountain Publishing Co., 1980

Mahler, C. B., *Once upon a Quilt*, van Nostrand Reinhold, Co., 1973

Marston, D. E., *Patchwork Today*, G. Bell & Sons, 1968

Marston, D. E., *Exploring Patchwork*, G. Bell & Sons, 1971

McCosh, B., *Introduction to Patchwork*, Mills & Boon, 1961

McKim, R. S., *One Hundred and One Patchwork Patterns*, Dover, 1962

Svennas, E., *Patchcraft*, van Nostrand Reinhold, Co., 1971

Timmins, A., *Introducing Patchwork*, B. T. Batsford Ltd., 1968

Index

The numbers in italics refer to illustration pages; **the numbers in bold refer to colour plates.**